my first maths book

David & Wendy Clemson

DORLING KINDERSLEY
London • New York • Stuttgart

A DORLING KINDERSLEY BOOK

Note to parents and teachers

My First Maths Book is a practical exploration of numbers, shapes, and patterns that will help you to introduce children to some fundamental concepts in mathematics.

By working through this book together, you can help your child to understand how maths is used in everyday life. Try to take every opportunity to show your child the relevance of maths at home or at school. Encourage your child to play with the puzzles and games in this book so that he or she can begin to take pleasure in thinking about mathematical ideas, and to view maths as fun.

It is important that children learn about number bonds, the names and characteristics of shapes, standard measures, and how to handle maths information, but also vital that they learn to use maths as an intellectual and practical tool. By prompting children to use their own methods for working things out, and their own words to voice their thoughts and suggestions, you can help them to realize that maths is not always about establishing one "right" answer.

Using the ideas in this book can help your child to gain confidence and positive feelings about maths that will lead to success in school work. More importantly, your child may discover mathematics to be profoundly enriching throughout his or her life.

David and Wendy Clemson

Project Editor Stella Love
Art Editor Sara Nunan

Managing Editor Jane Yorke
Managing Art Editor Chris Scollen
Production Paola Fagherazzi
Photography by Steve Gorton and Alex Wilson

First published in Great Britain in 1994
by Dorling Kindersley Limited,
9 Henrietta Street, London WC2E 8PS

Reprinted 1997

Visit us on the World Wide Web at
http://www.dk.com

A CIP catalogue record for this book is available from the British Library.

ISBN 0-7513-5129-6

Reproduced by Colourscan, Singapore
Printed and bound in Italy by L.E.G.O.

Contents

6	7	8	9	10
16	17	18	19	20
26	27	28	29	30
36	37	38	39	40
46	47	48	49	50

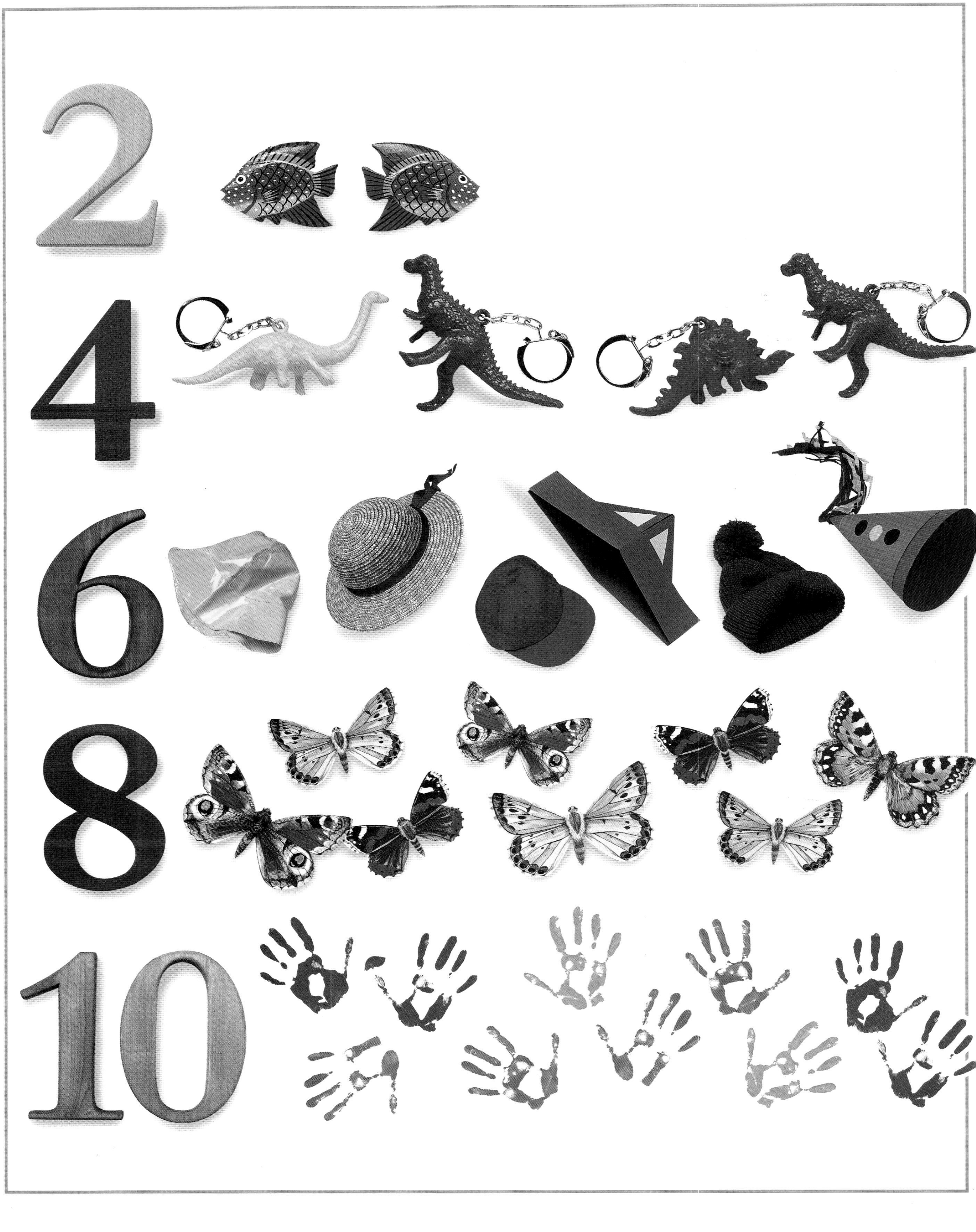
2
4
6
8
10

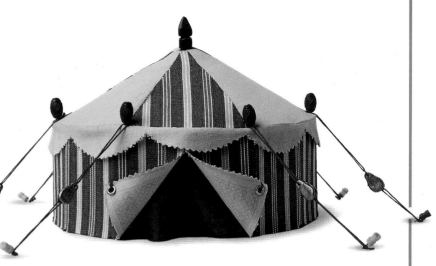

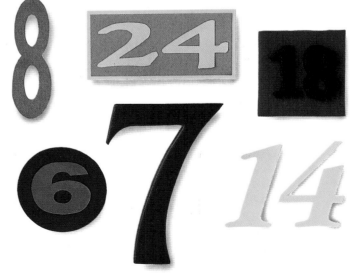

Sorting

Can you sort things into **sets**, or groups? Try these puzzles and find out which things belong together.

Hat shop

The hat shop has a hat for every occasion.

Which hats would you wear at a party?

Which hats would you wear in cold or wet weather?

How many hats are for wearing in the sun?

Button box

How many green buttons are there?
How many buttons are round?

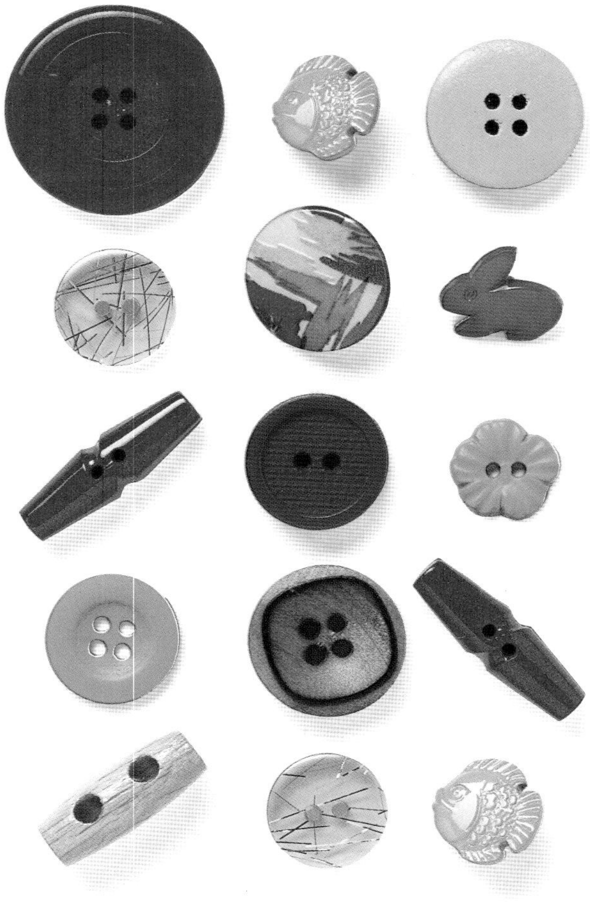

Can you find the buttons with more than two holes?

Backpack

Only four things will fit into the backpack. Which things will you pack to go swimming?

shoes

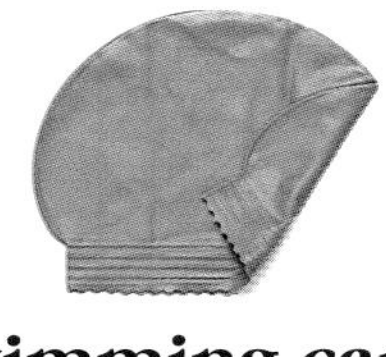

swimming cap

ball

goggles

slippers

towel

shorts

swimming costume

sports shirt

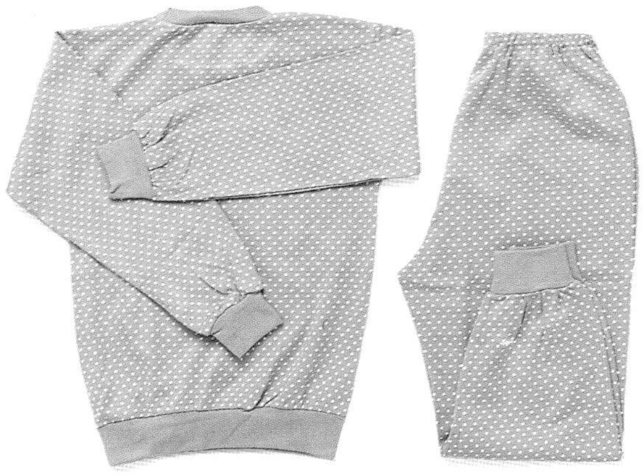

pyjamas

wash bag

Which four things will you pack to stay at a friend's house? What will you leave behind if you go to play in the park?

Fasteners

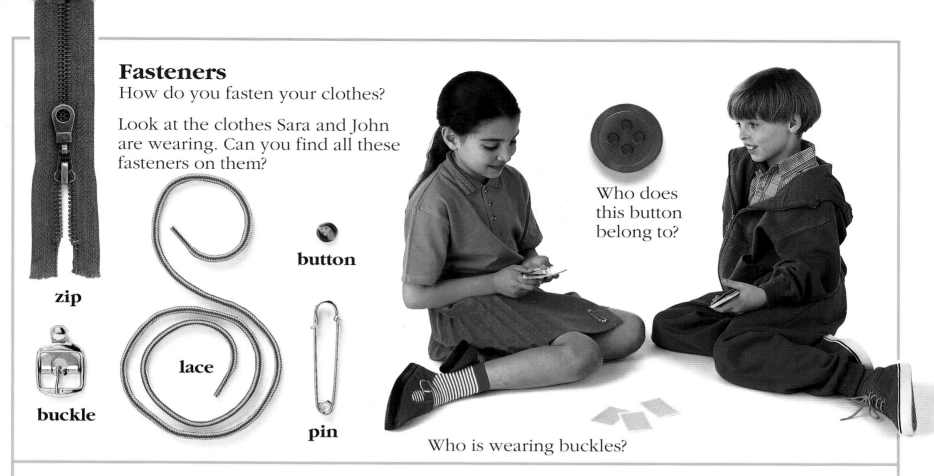

How do you fasten your clothes?

Look at the clothes Sara and John are wearing. Can you find all these fasteners on them?

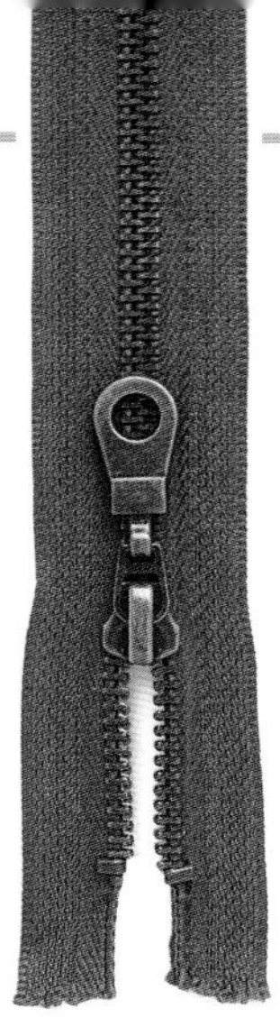

zip

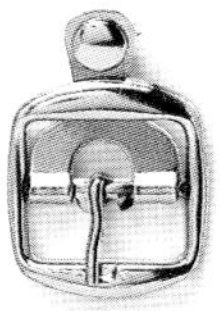

buckle

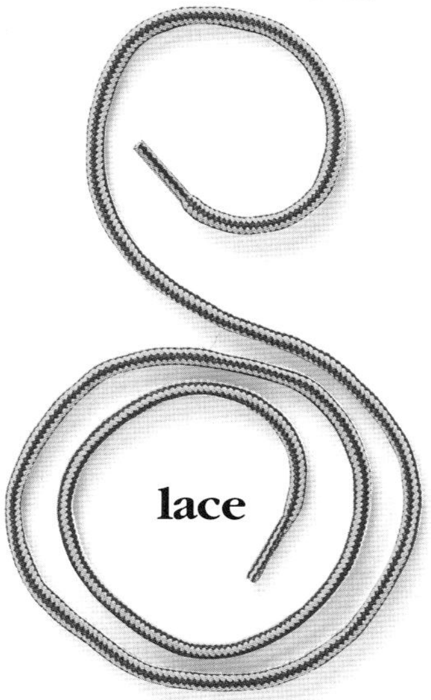

lace

button

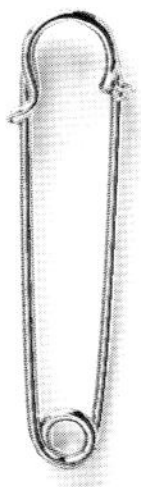

pin

Who does this button belong to?

Who is wearing buckles?

Outfits

Daniel has these clothes hanging in his wardrobe. Can you help him choose what to put on?

How many different outfits can Daniel wear? Remember to count the trousers and shirt he is already wearing.

If one of Daniel's shirts gets dirty, how many possible outfits are left?

Adding up and taking away

Remind yourself of what you know about adding up and taking away.

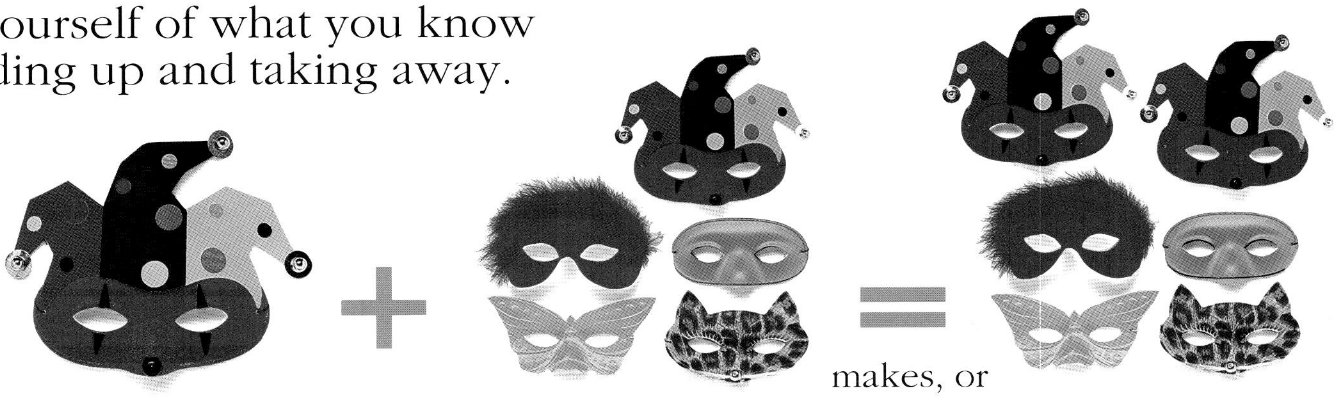

2 eye-holes **add** 10 eye-holes makes, or is **equal to** 12 eye-holes

Adding up

Using the eye-holes of the masks to count with, you can make these adding up sums, or **additions**.

$2 + 10 = 12$

$12 = 2 + 10$

$10 + 2 = 12$

Taking away

Now look at these take aways, or **subtractions**.

12 eye-holes **take away** 10 eye-holes leaves, or is **equal to** 2 eye-holes

$12 - 2 = 10$

$10 = 12 - 2$

$10 - 2 = 8$

0 1 2 3 4 5 6 7 8 9 10

Missing numbers

Use the number line at the bottom of the page to help you with these additions and subtractions.

Can you find out what the missing numbers should be?

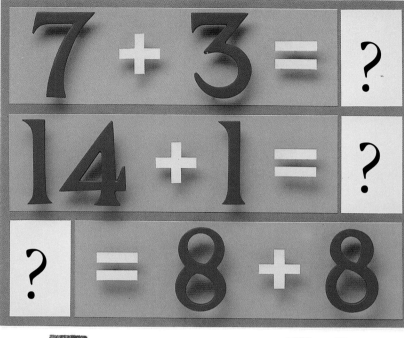

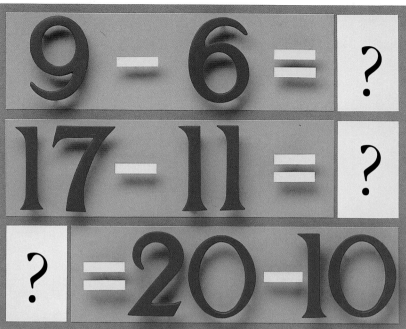

7 + 3 = ?

14 + 1 = ?

? = 8 + 8

9 – 6 = ?

17 – 11 = ?

? = 20 – 10

5 + ? = 11

5 + ? = 12

12 – ? = 5

16 – ? = 7

? + 13 = 16

? + 20 = 20

? – 9 = 12

? – 1 = 15

Which number is missing from this line of frogs?

What happens if you put 9 in the line instead of 13?

5 + 2 + 13 – ? = 5

? = 6 + 11 – 8 – 3 + 4 + 1

What happens if you put 5 instead of 11 in the line, and 2 instead of 8?

11 12 13 14 15 16 17 18 19 20

Counting number groups

Try these counting puzzles and practise adding up number groups. Use the number line at the bottom of the page to help you.

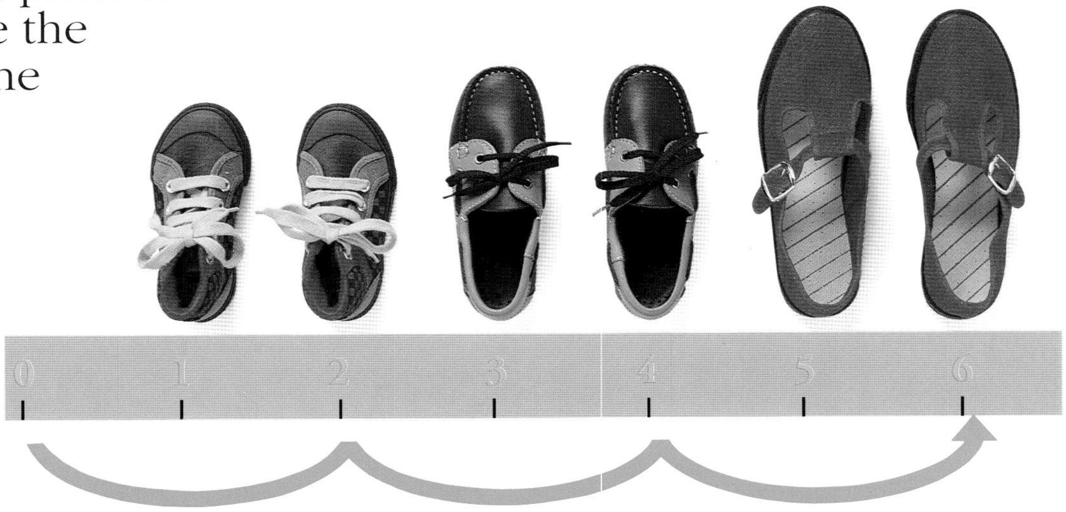

Groups of two
Can you add up in twos and count the number of shoes?

Groups of three
Add up these cherries in threes. Can you carry on counting up in threes?

Groups of four
Can you count up the legs of these animals in fours?

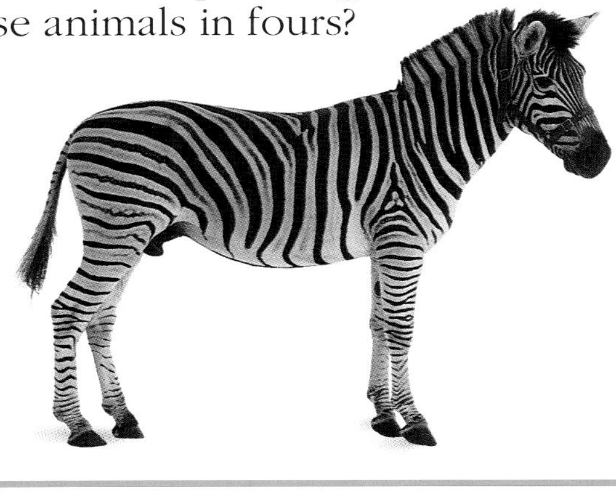

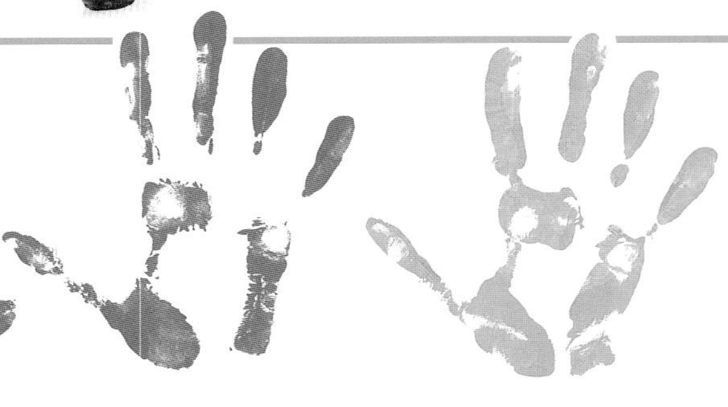

Groups of five
Try counting up the fingers in fives.

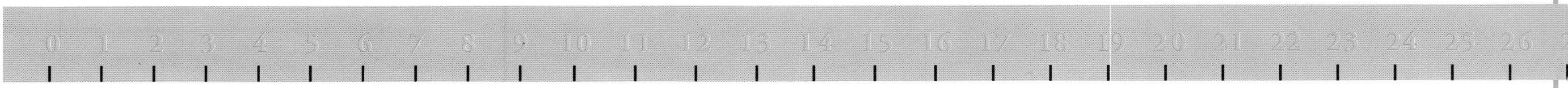

Groups of six

How many pencils are there? Count them in sixes.

Groups of seven

What number can you count up to in groups of seven? Use the number line to help you.

Groups of eight

Count up in eights along the number line and write the numbers down. Can you see a pattern in the numbers?

Groups of nine

How many groups of nine cars are there in 36 cars?

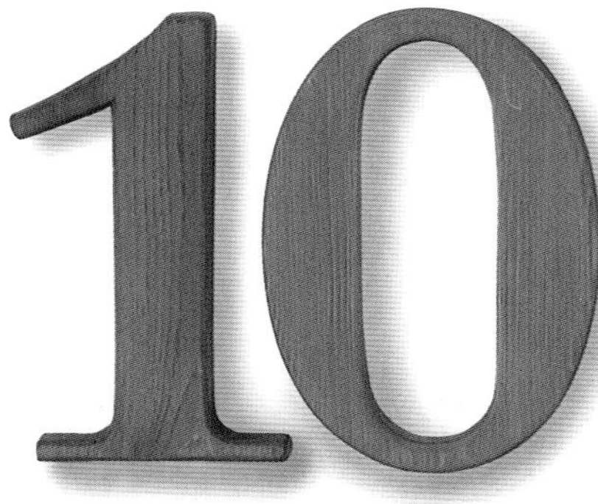

Groups of ten

If you had 50 skittles, how many groups of 10 would you have?

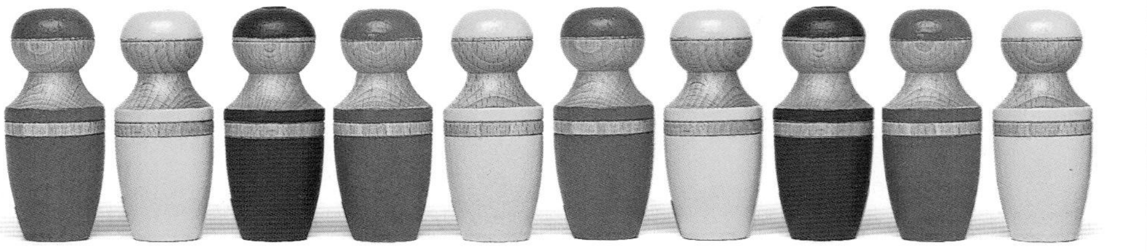

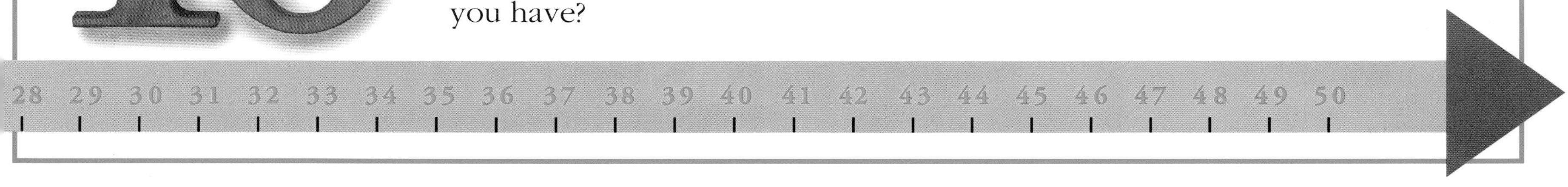

One hundred square

Use the hundred square number board on the opposite page to solve these puzzles.

Twos

The pattern of counting in twos is shown in red.

The numbers on red squares are called even numbers.

All the others are odd numbers. Is 18 odd or even?

Threes

Trace the pattern of threes on the number board with your finger.

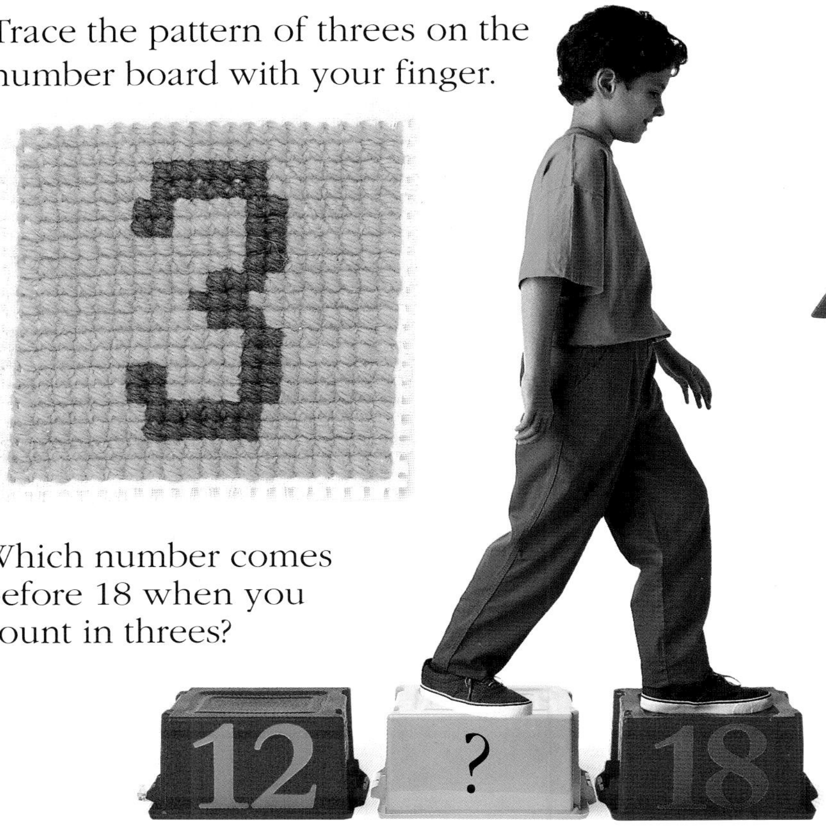

Which number comes before 18 when you count in threes?

Fours

Put buttons on the pattern of fours. How many buttons do you need?

Nines

Which numbers are missing from the pattern of nines below?

Add together the **digits** of 18.
1 + 8 = 9

What happens if you add the digits of other nine-pattern numbers in the same way?

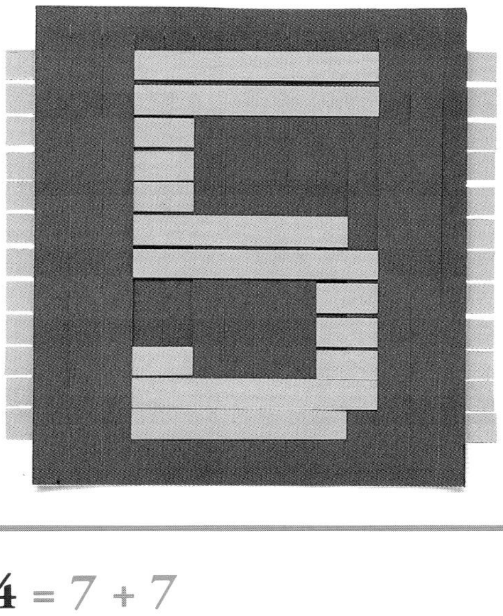

Fives

Can you count in fives using the number board?

How many numbers are shown in the five pattern?

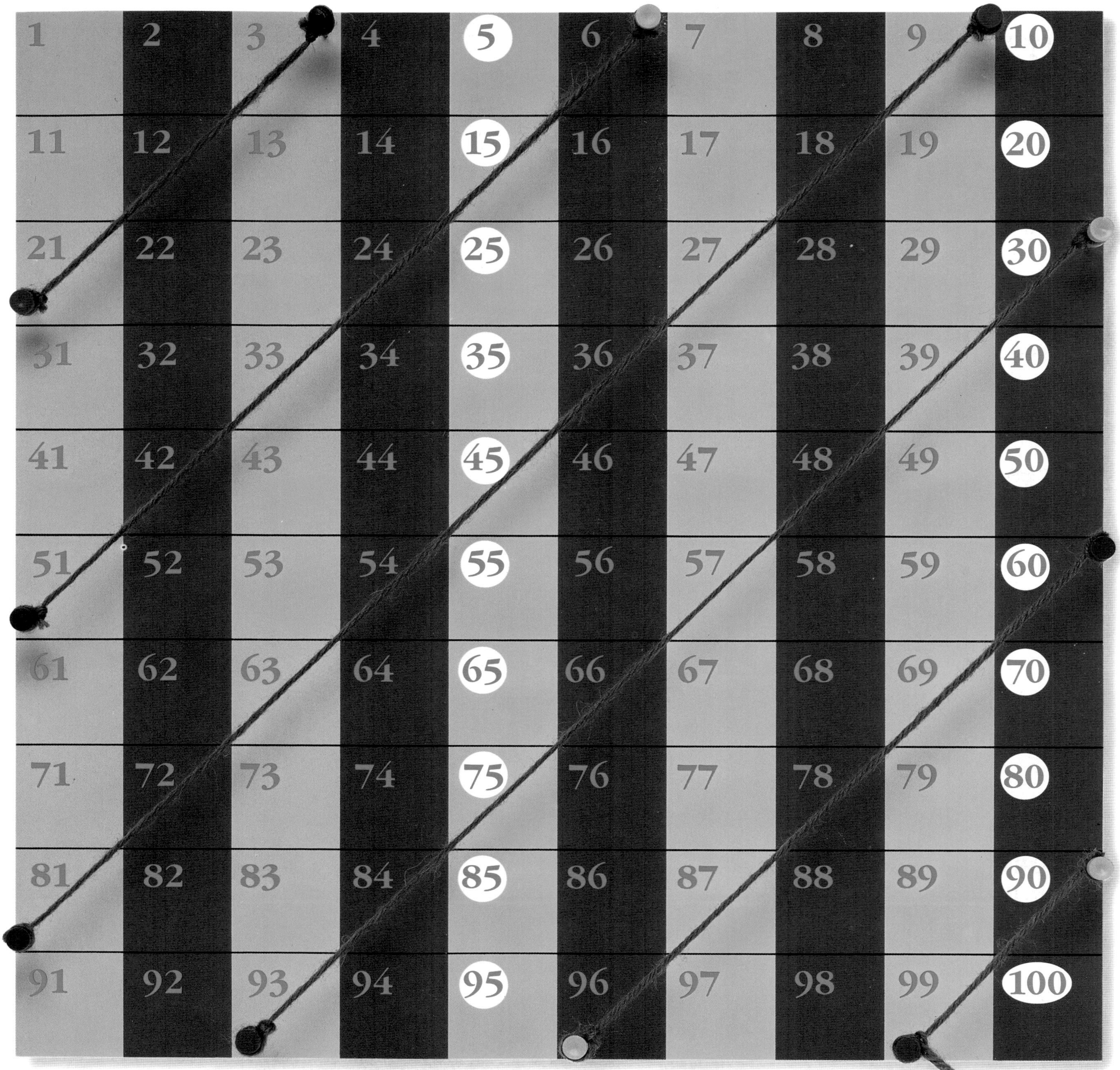

Twos, fives, and tens

Twenty fits in the patterns of twos, fives, and tens. Can you find other numbers belonging in more than one pattern?

Multiplying

Can you work out the answers to these **multiplications**? Use the pictures and the number line to help you.

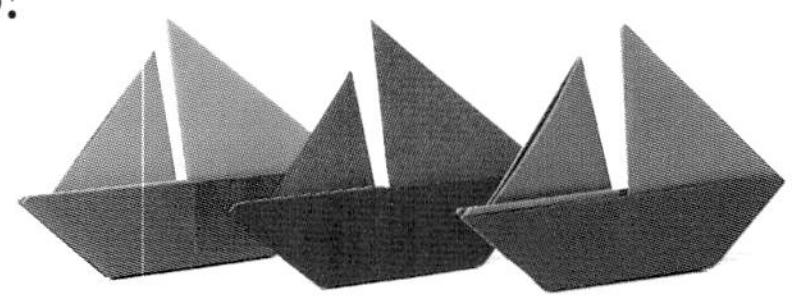

Sailing boats

Here are 3 lots of 2 boats, which makes 6 boats altogether.

3 x 2 = 6

In numbers and **symbols** we write it like this. This symbol means **lots of**, or **multiply by**.

Fish

Here are 3 lots of 4 fish. How many fish are there altogether?

3 x 4 = ?

Starfish

Here are 2 lots of 5 starfish. How many starfish are there?

2 x 5 = ?

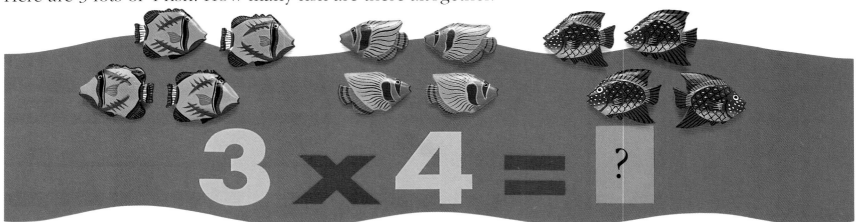

0 1 2 3 4 5 6 7 8 9 10 11 12 13 14 15 16 17 18 19 20 21 22 23 24 25 26 2

Anchors

How many anchors are there?

1 x 7 = ?

Pebbles and shells

How many pebbles do 5 lots of 5 pebbles make?

5 x 5 = ?

How many shells do 2 lots of 10 shells make?

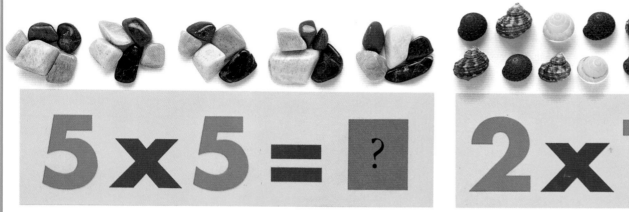

2 x 10 = ?

Shell puzzle

These shell numbers are missing from the multiplications below. Where do they belong?

? = 5 × 4

10 × ? = 50

? = 4 × 5

? × 2 = 22

2 × 2 × 2 = ?

28 29 30 31 32 33 34 35 36 37 38 39 40 41 42 43 44 45 46 47 48 49 50

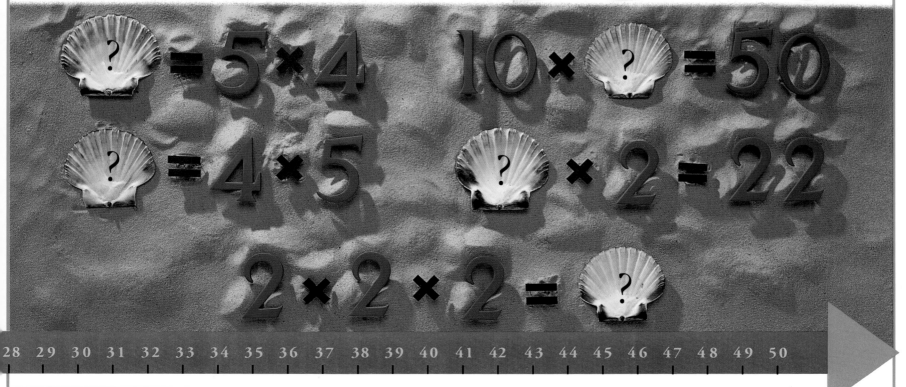

Sharing out

Can you share out all the things shown on these pages so that everyone has an equal share?

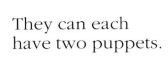

They can each have two puppets.

Finger puppets

There are six finger puppets to be shared out between Tessa, Rose, and Joe.

Animal badges

Try sharing out these animal badges between Tessa, Rose, and Joe.

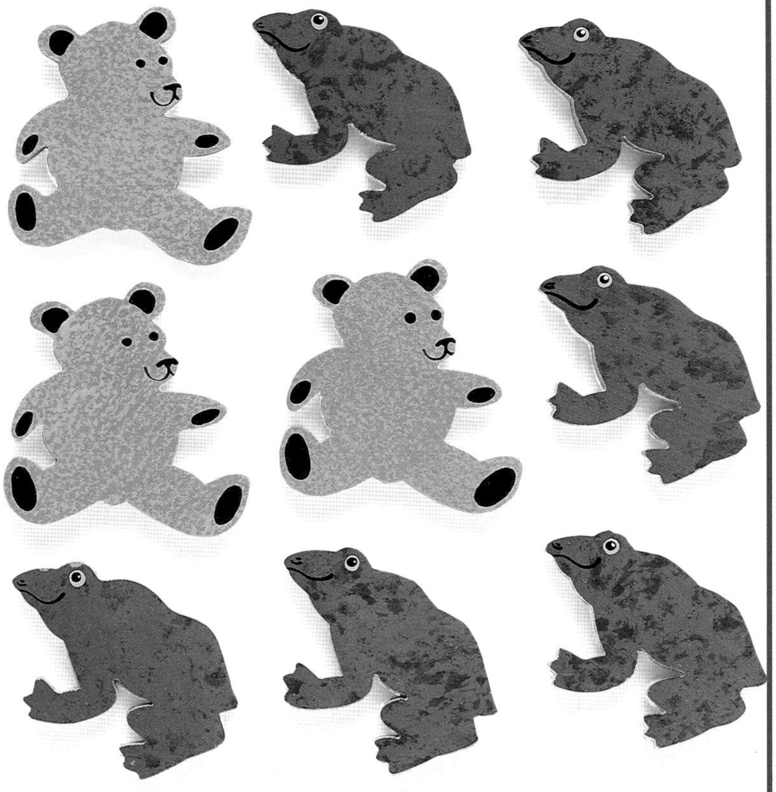

How many badges can each person have? How many frog badges will each person get?

Butterflies

Can you share out the paper butterflies between the three children?

Key-rings
How many people can have five key-rings?

Pencils and rubbers
How many people can have one pencil and one rubber each?

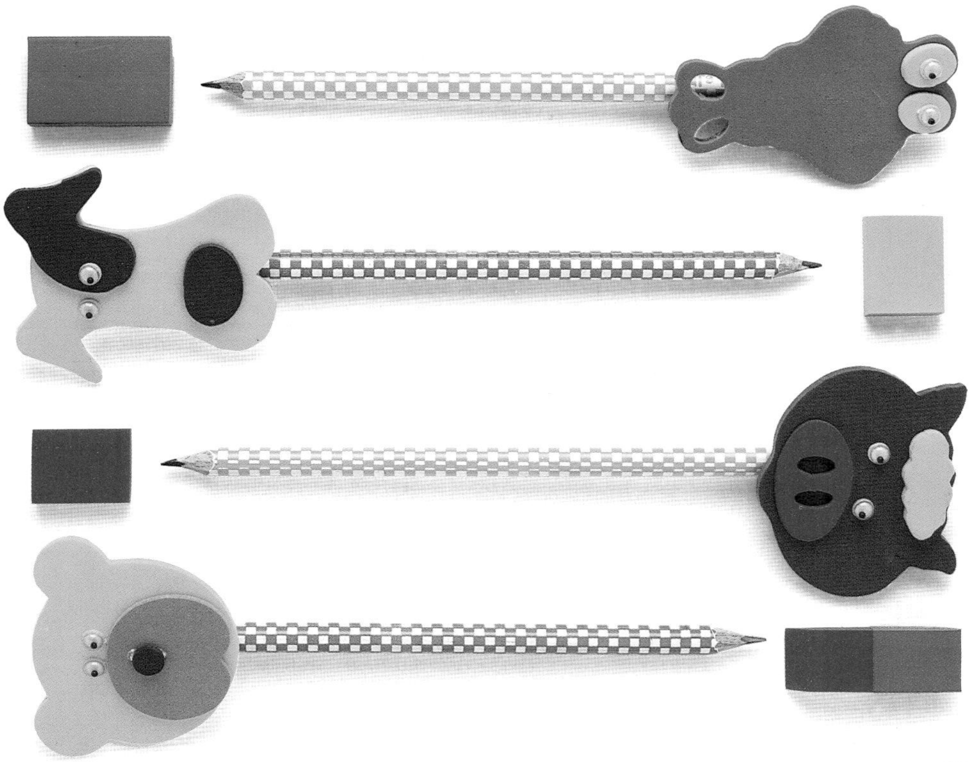

Presents
How many people can have two presents each?

If ten people share these presents, how many will each person have?

Zoo tickets
Here are some tickets for the zoo. How many people can go to see the animals?

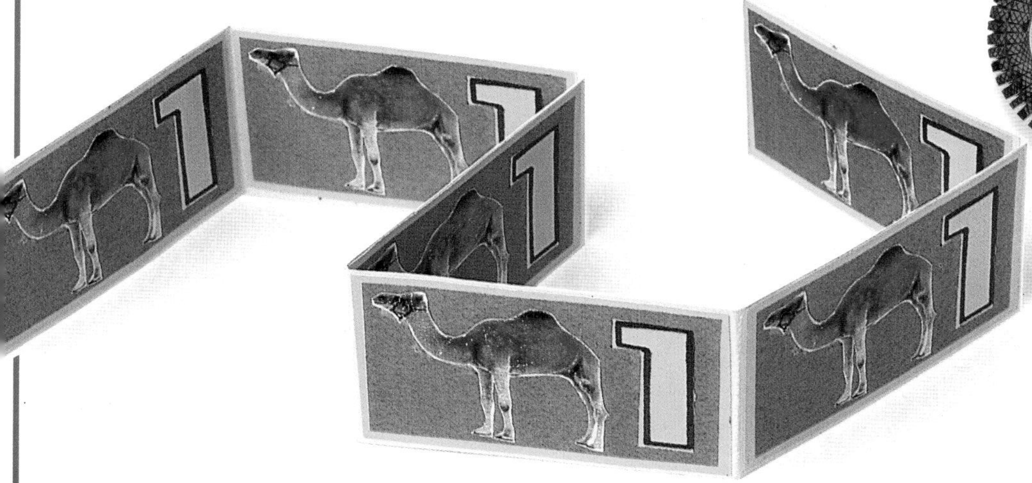

Dividing

Here are some more sharing out, or **division** problems for you to try.

Missing drinks

Four children have one sandwich each but their drinks have been forgotten. How many drinks are needed?

Fruit tarts

There are eight fruit tarts, so four children can have two each. We can also write this in numbers and symbols.

This means shared between, or **divided by**.

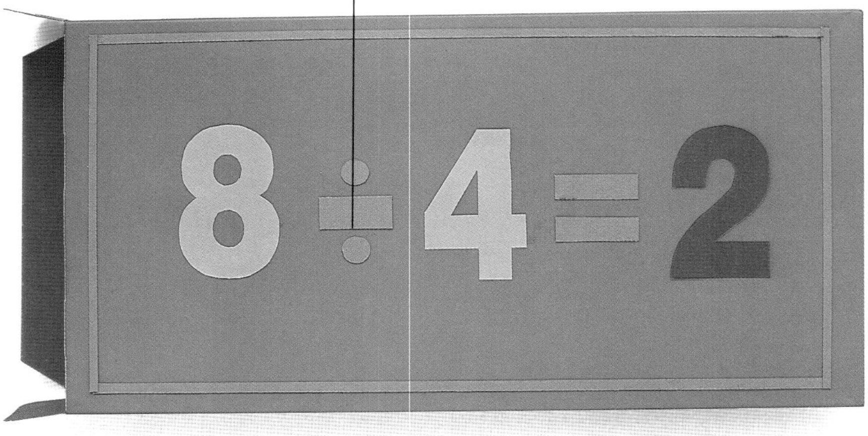

8 tarts shared between 4 children makes 2 tarts each.

Nutty nibbles

How many nuts are there altogether? How many nuts can each of the four children have?

Picnic time

Five people go on a picnic and share out the food. Sharing the sandwiches can be written like this.

$$20 \div 5 = 4$$

Can you match the division puzzles below with each of the picnic things and share them out equally?

$5 \div 5 =$?

$15 \div 5 =$?

$10 \div 5 =$?

$25 \div 5 =$?

$10 \div 2 =$?

$9 \div$? $= 3$

$18 \div 3 =$?

$12 \div$? $= 2$

$20 \div 10 =$?

$16 \div$? $= 4$

Orange puzzle

Can you work out the answers to these divisions?

Use the line of oranges below to help you.

Shapes and patterns

All shapes have names to describe them. Patterns can be made by putting different shapes together.

Flat shapes

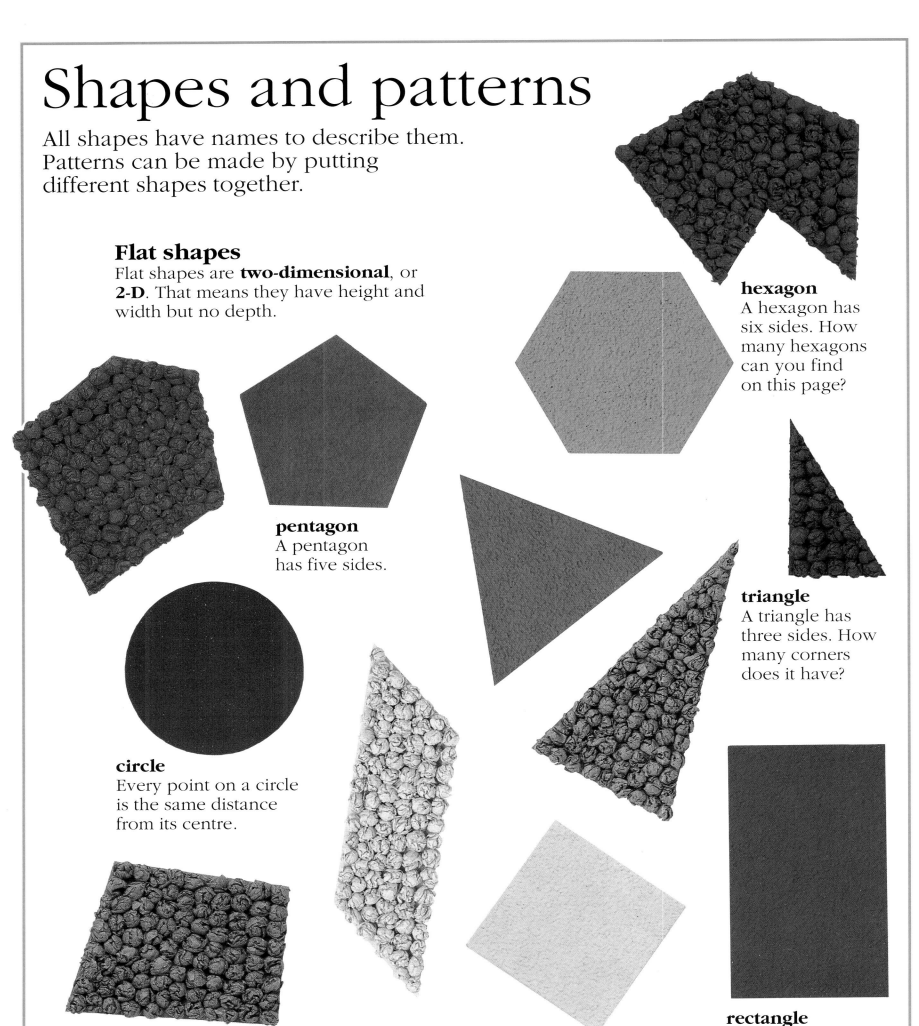

Flat shapes are **two-dimensional**, or **2-D**. That means they have height and width but no depth.

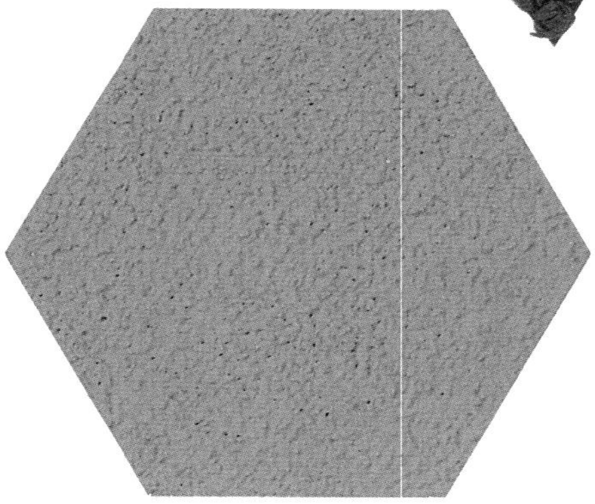

hexagon
A hexagon has six sides. How many hexagons can you find on this page?

pentagon
A pentagon has five sides.

triangle
A triangle has three sides. How many corners does it have?

circle
Every point on a circle is the same distance from its centre.

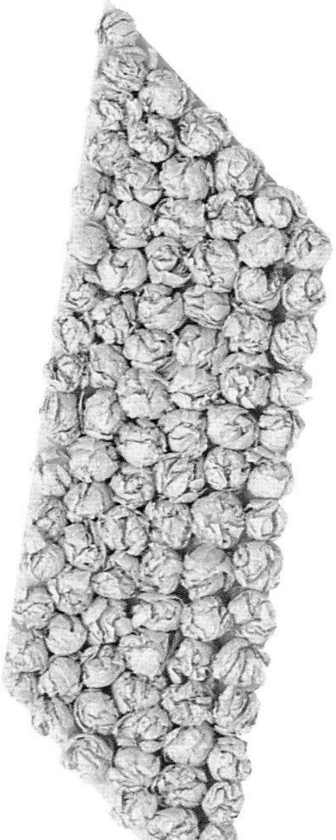

quadrilateral
A quadrilateral is a shape with four sides. How many quadrilaterals can you find on this page?

square
A square has four equal sides and four corners that match.

rectangle
A rectangle has two pairs of matching sides and four corners that match.

Shape puzzle

With four squares you can make five different patterns like this. Cut out five paper squares and triangles.

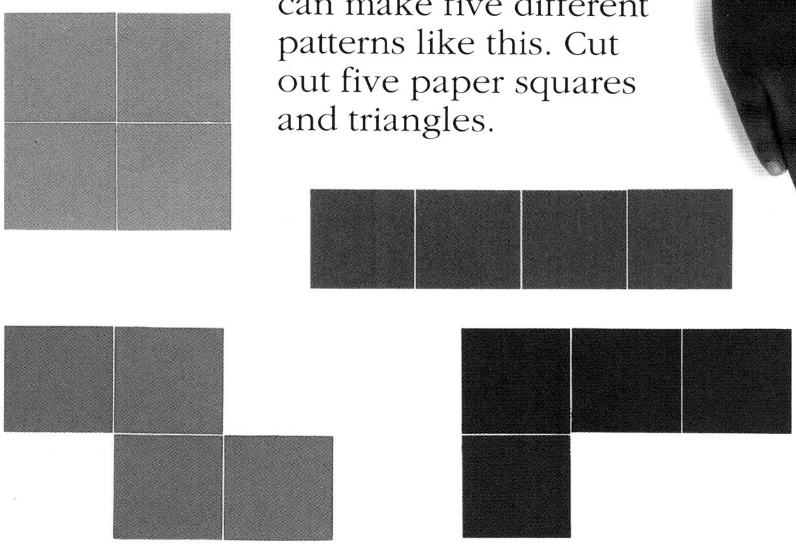

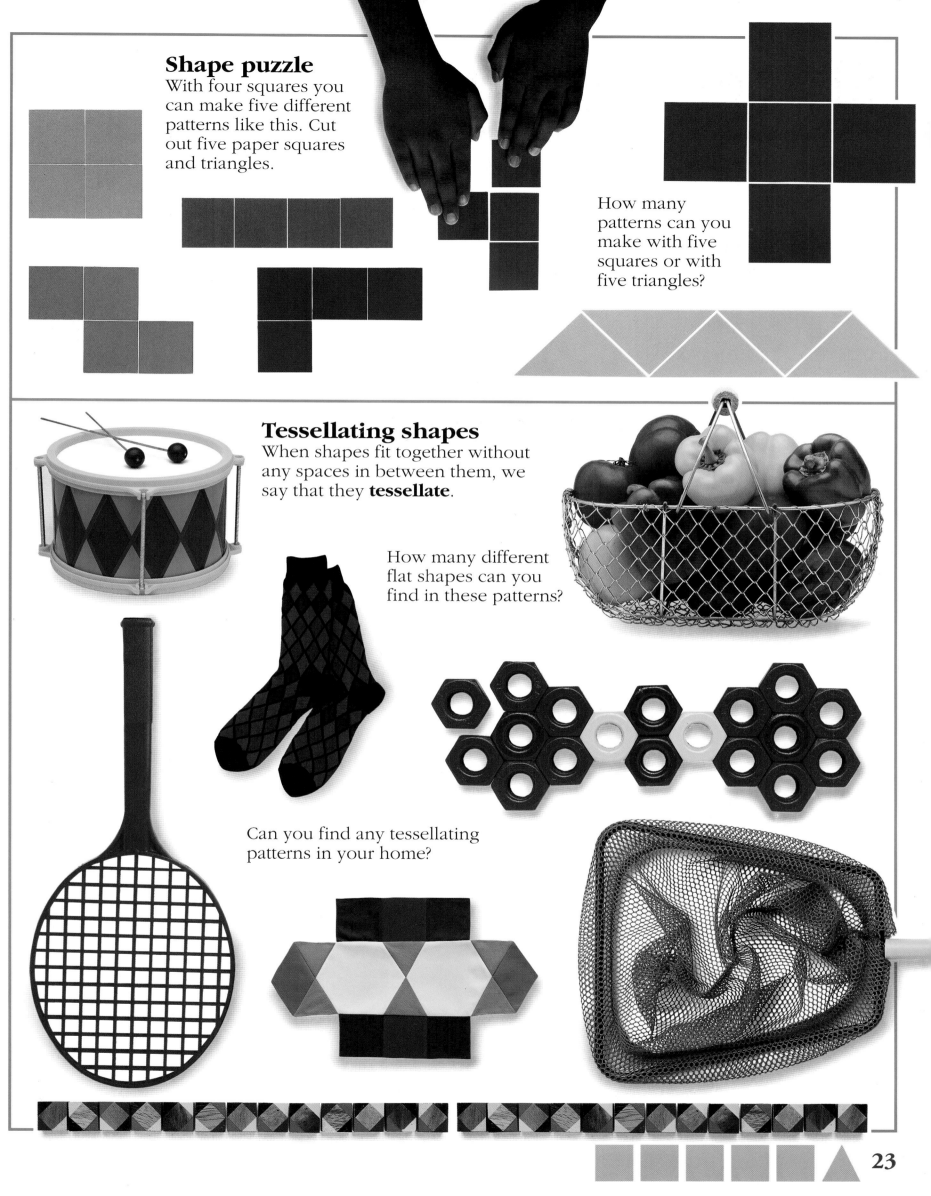

How many patterns can you make with five squares or with five triangles?

Tessellating shapes

When shapes fit together without any spaces in between them, we say that they **tessellate**.

How many different flat shapes can you find in these patterns?

Can you find any tessellating patterns in your home?

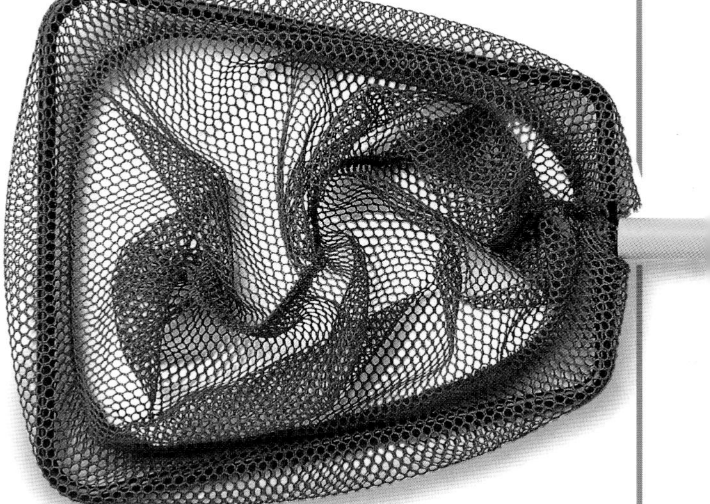

Solid shapes

Solid and hollow shapes are described as **three-dimensional**, or **3-D**. A flat part of a 3-D shape is called a **face**.

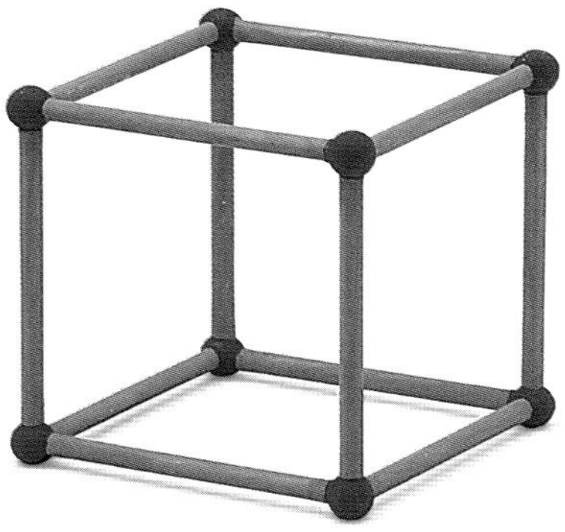

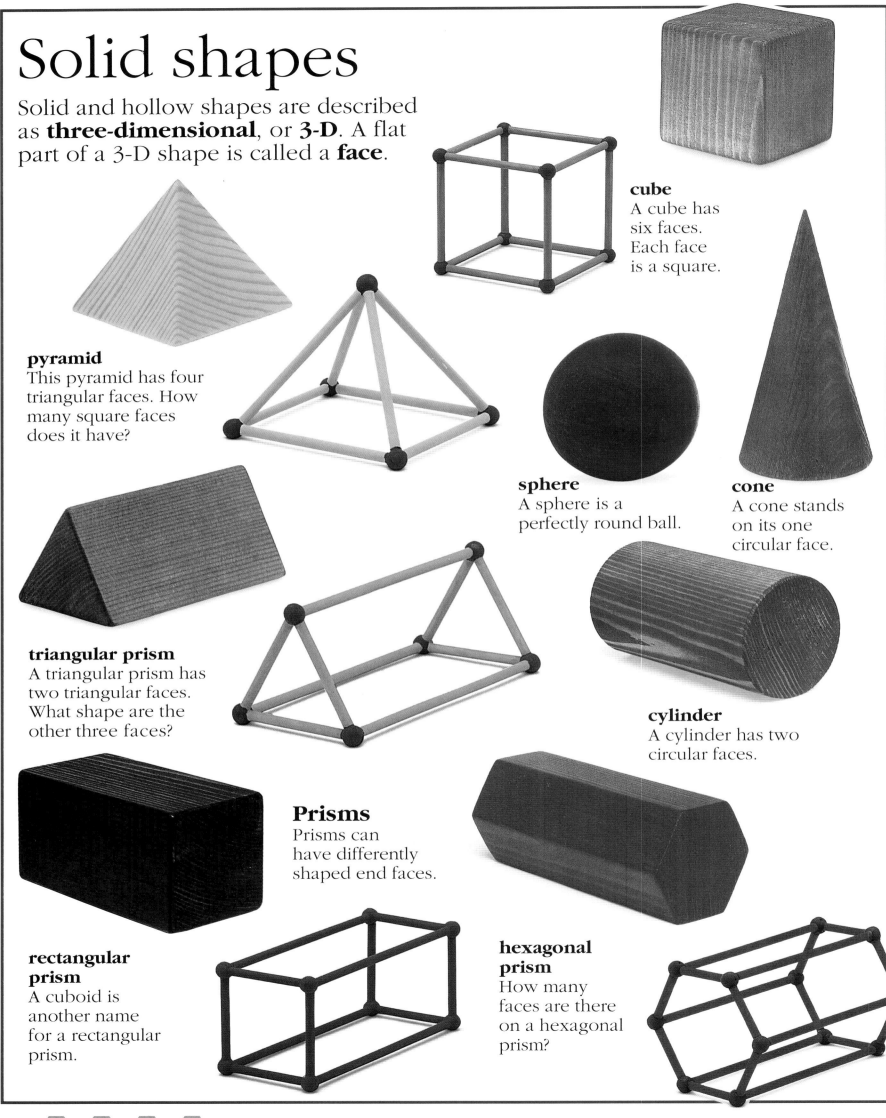

cube
A cube has six faces. Each face is a square.

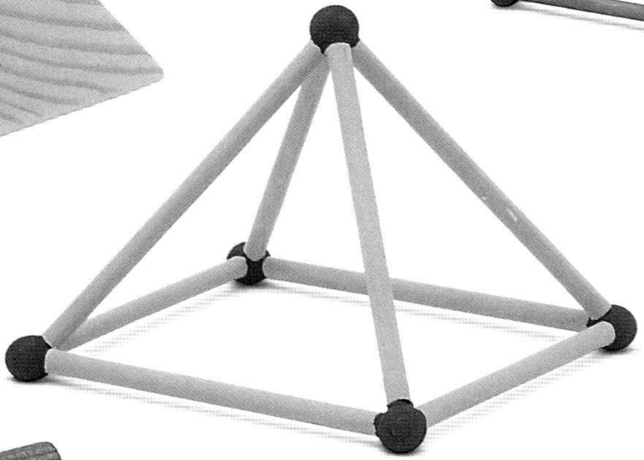

pyramid
This pyramid has four triangular faces. How many square faces does it have?

sphere
A sphere is a perfectly round ball.

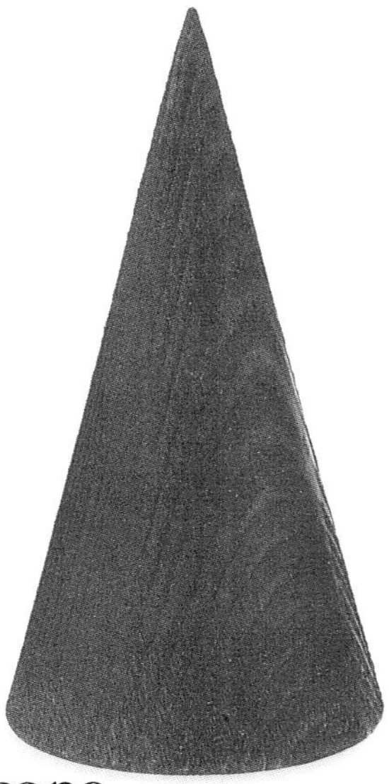

cone
A cone stands on its one circular face.

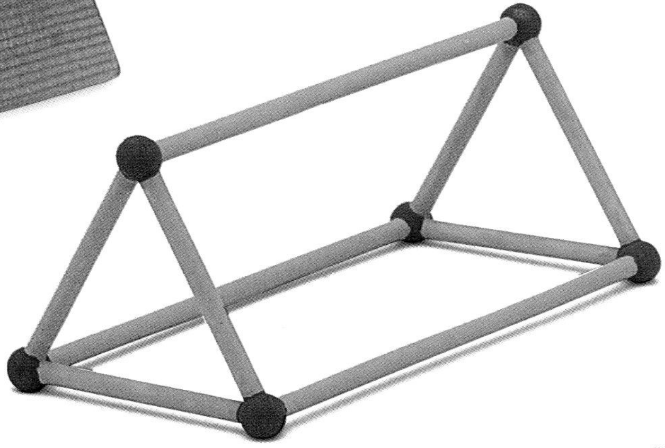

triangular prism
A triangular prism has two triangular faces. What shape are the other three faces?

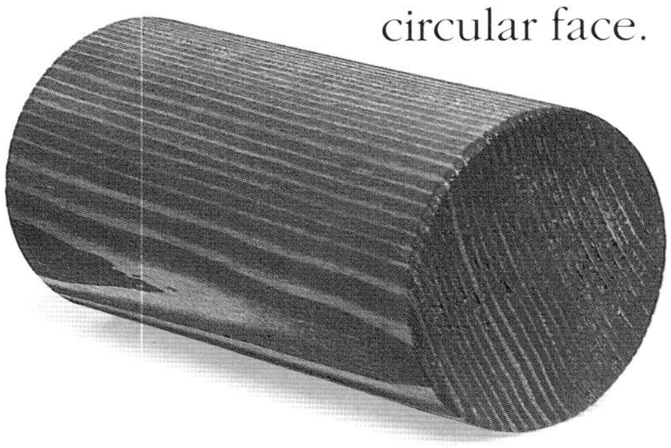

cylinder
A cylinder has two circular faces.

Prisms
Prisms can have differently shaped end faces.

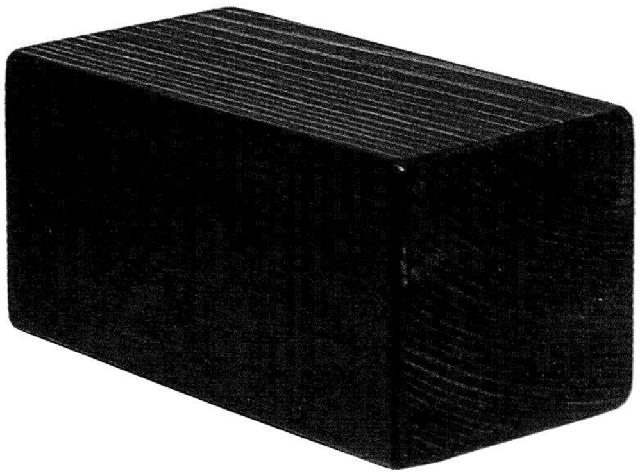

rectangular prism
A cuboid is another name for a rectangular prism.

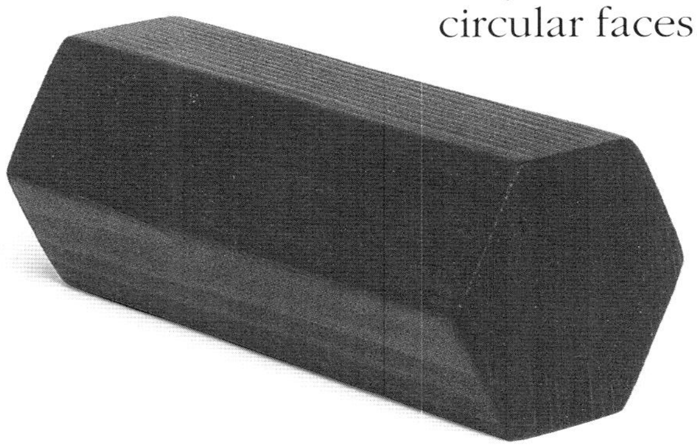
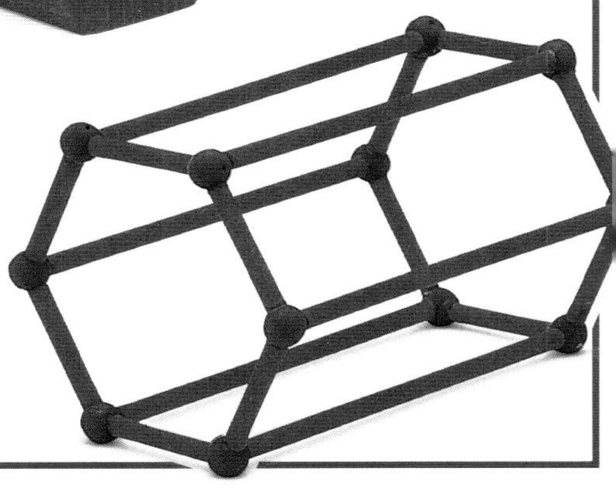

hexagonal prism
How many faces are there on a hexagonal prism?

Nets

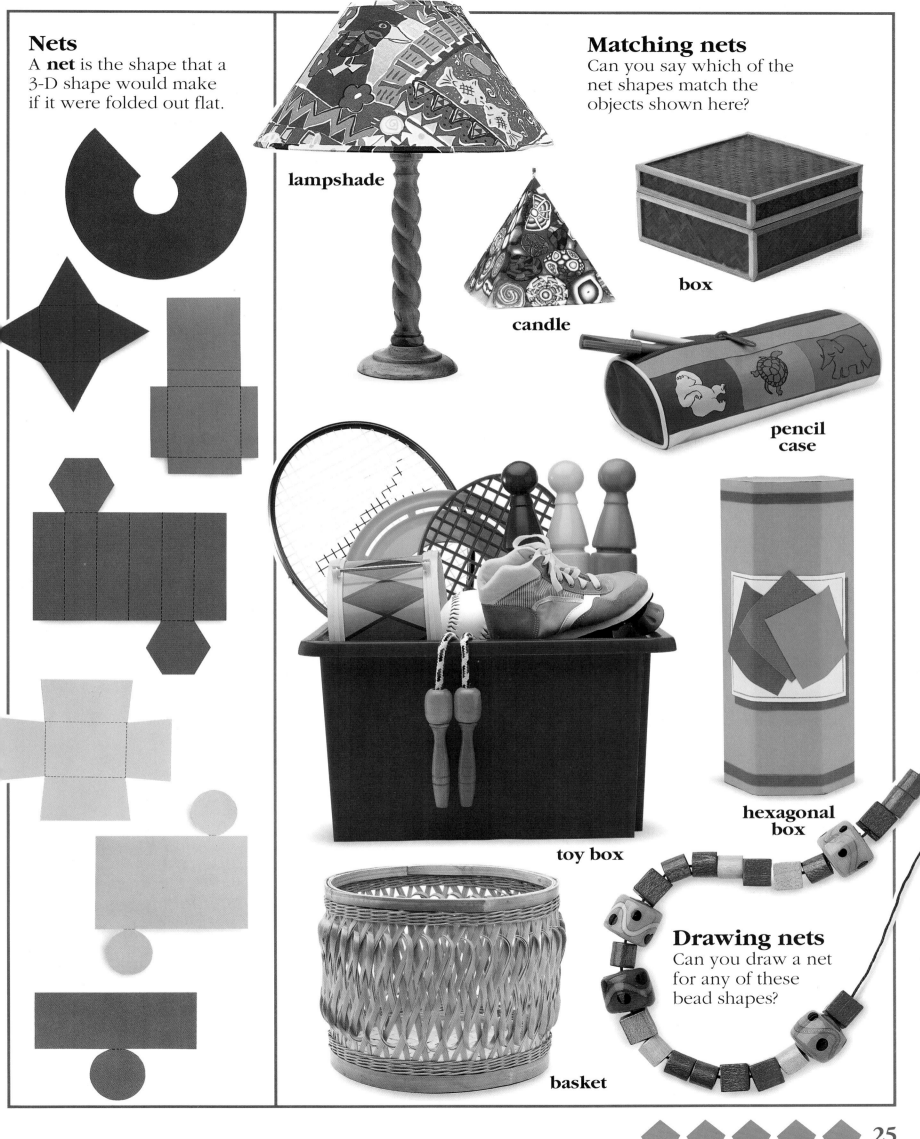

A **net** is the shape that a 3-D shape would make if it were folded out flat.

Matching nets

Can you say which of the net shapes match the objects shown here?

lampshade

candle

box

pencil case

toy box

hexagonal box

basket

Drawing nets

Can you draw a net for any of these bead shapes?

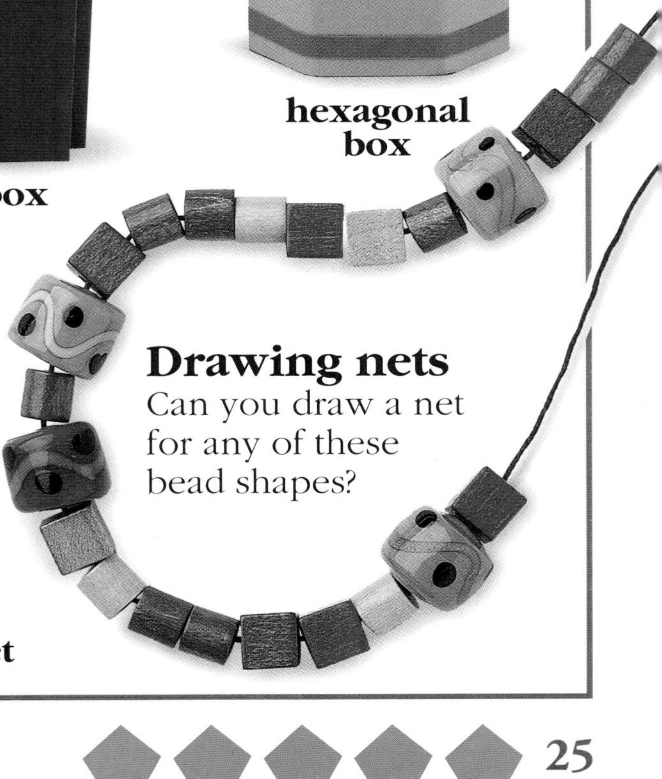

Measuring length

Measuring tools can be long or short, bendy or straight, for different measuring jobs.

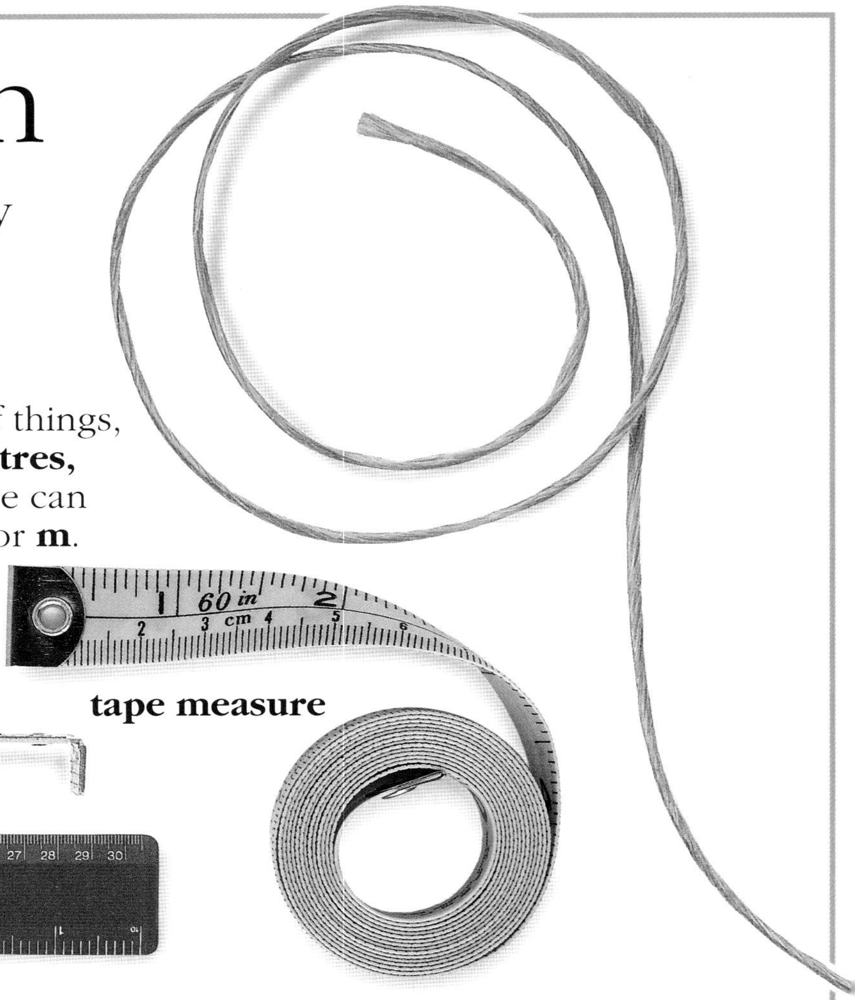

Measures

We measure the length of things, in **millimetres**, **centimetres,** and **metres**. For short, we can write these as **mm**, **cm**, or **m**.

tape measure

steel rule

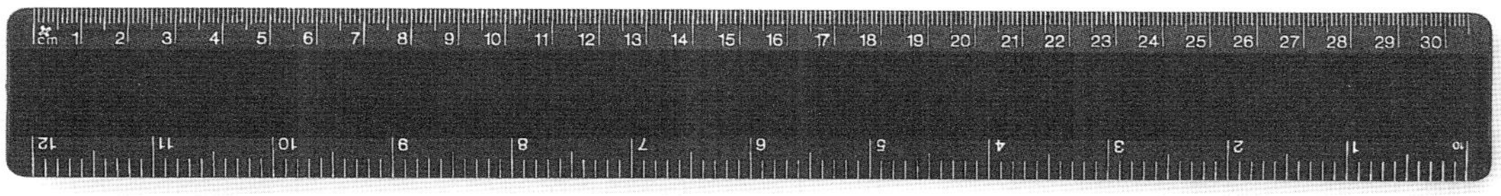

ruler

Measuring people

Can you measure a friend's waist with a piece of string and a ruler?

With a friend, measure how tall you are. Who is the taller?

Can you measure the length of one stride?

How far can you jump?

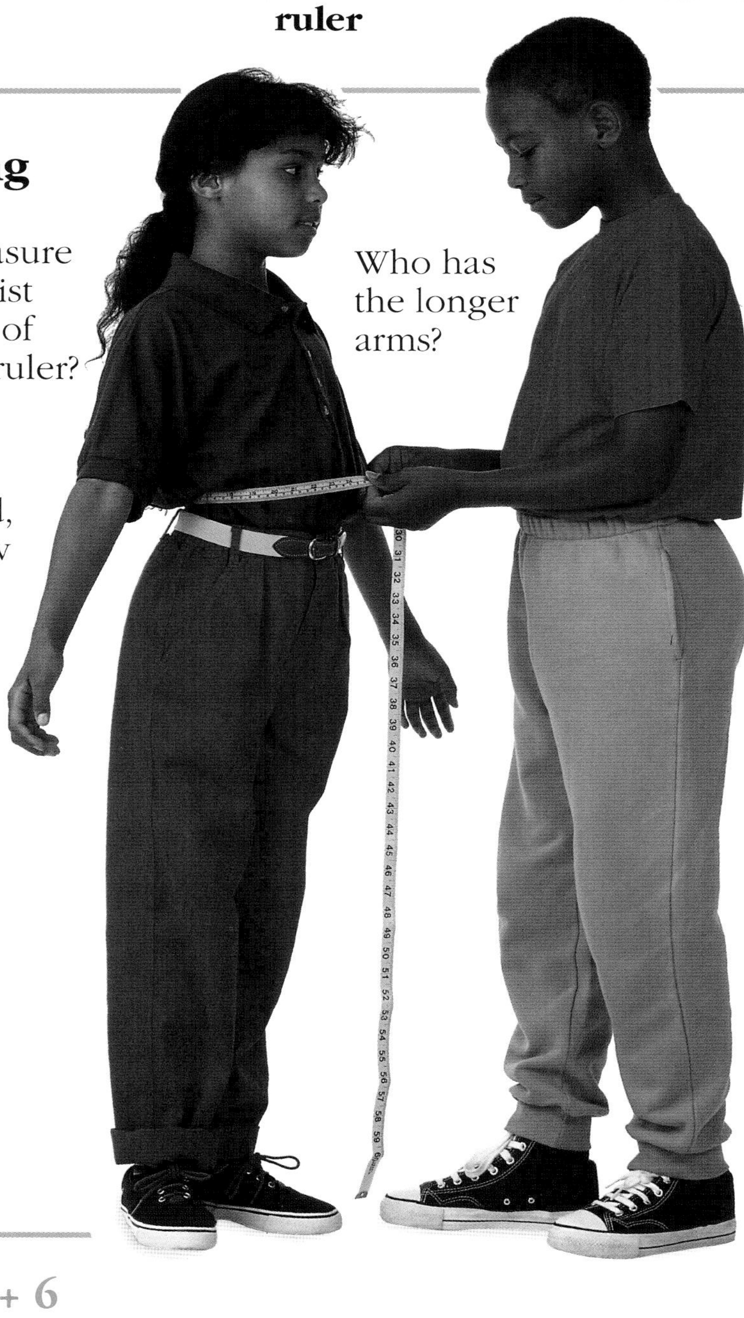

Who has the longer arms?

Circumference

The length all the way round an object is called the **circumference**.

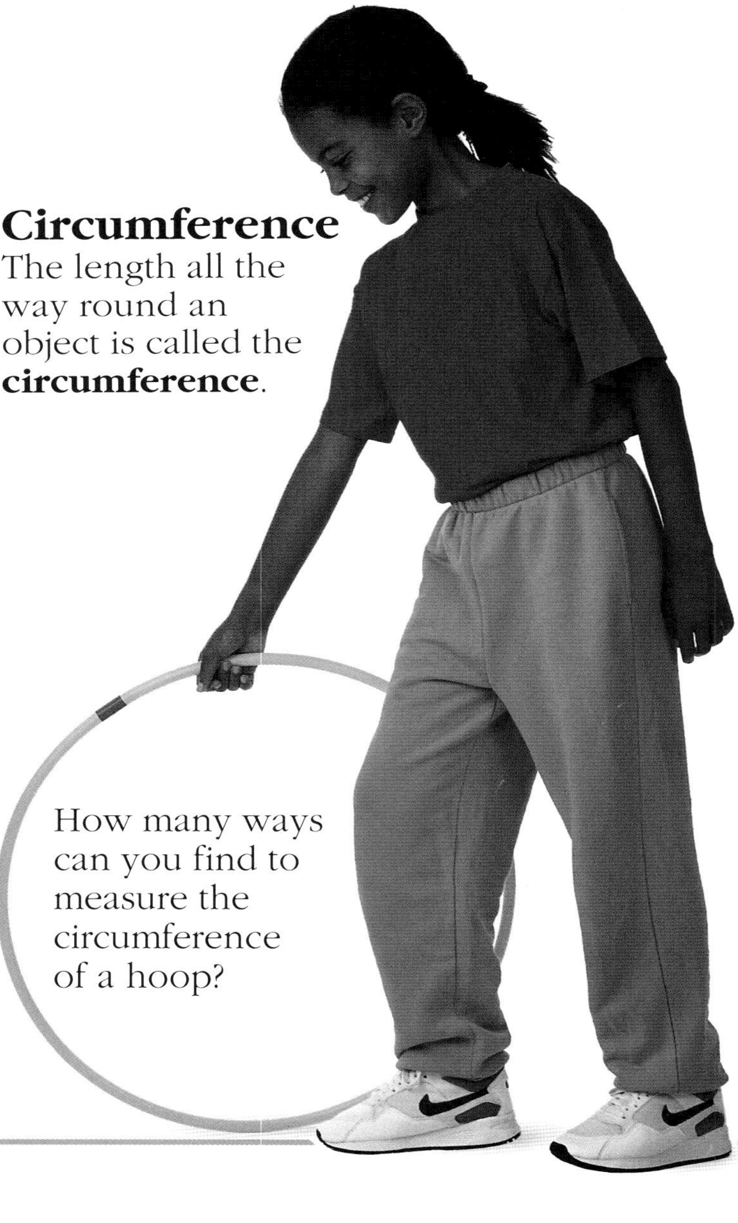

How many ways can you find to measure the circumference of a hoop?

crayon

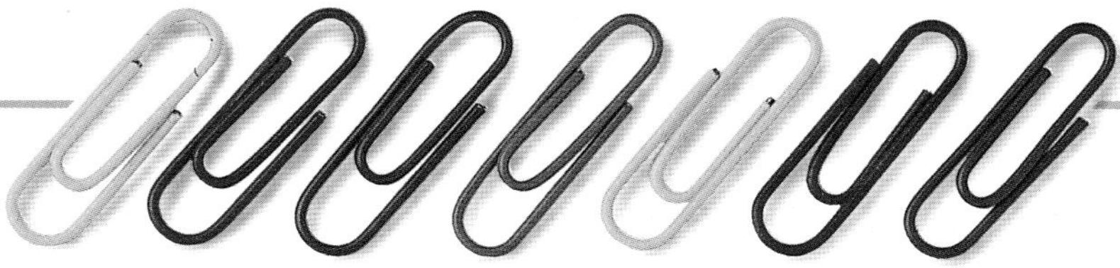

paper-clips

Measuring puzzles

What tools will you use to measure the things on this page?

How long are seven paper-clips end to end?

pen

Is the pen longer than the scissors?

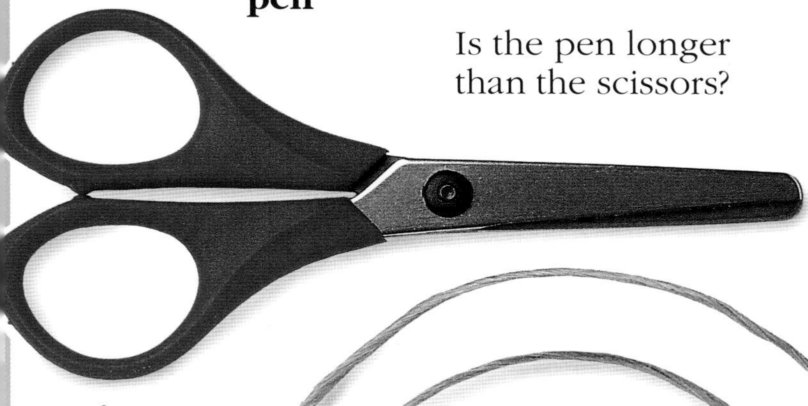

scissors

bendy pen

Will the bendy pen fit into the pencil case?

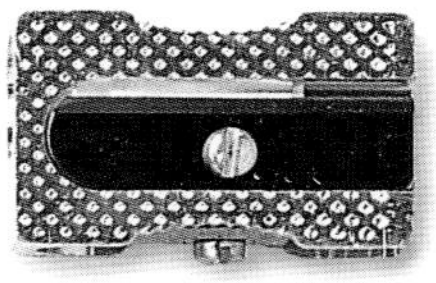

pencil sharpener

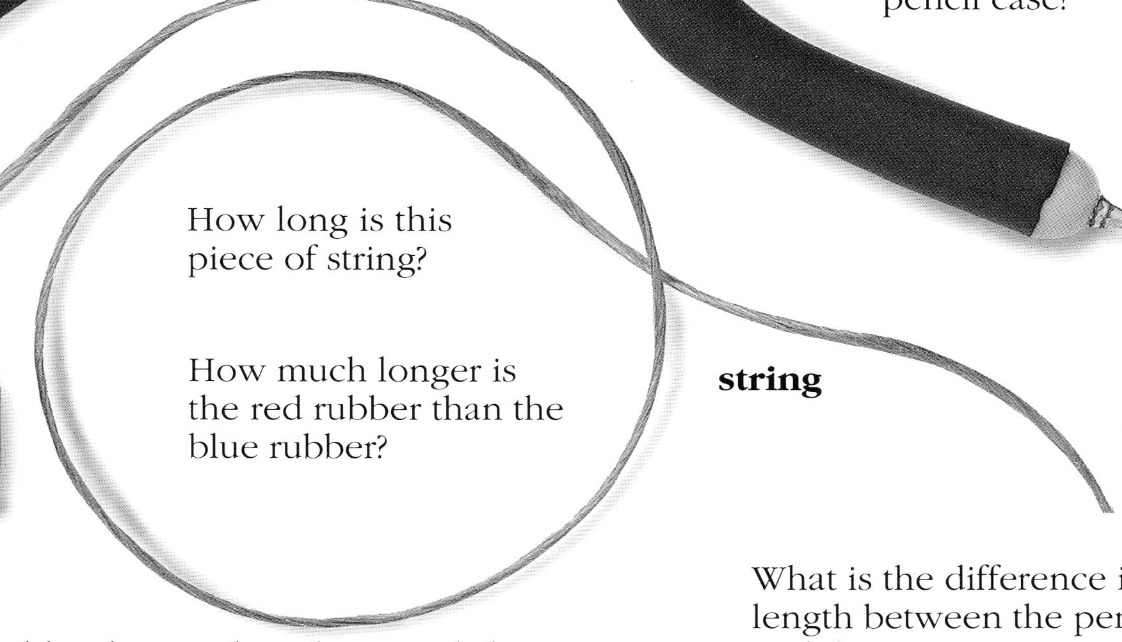

string

How long is this piece of string?

How much longer is the red rubber than the blue rubber?

rubber

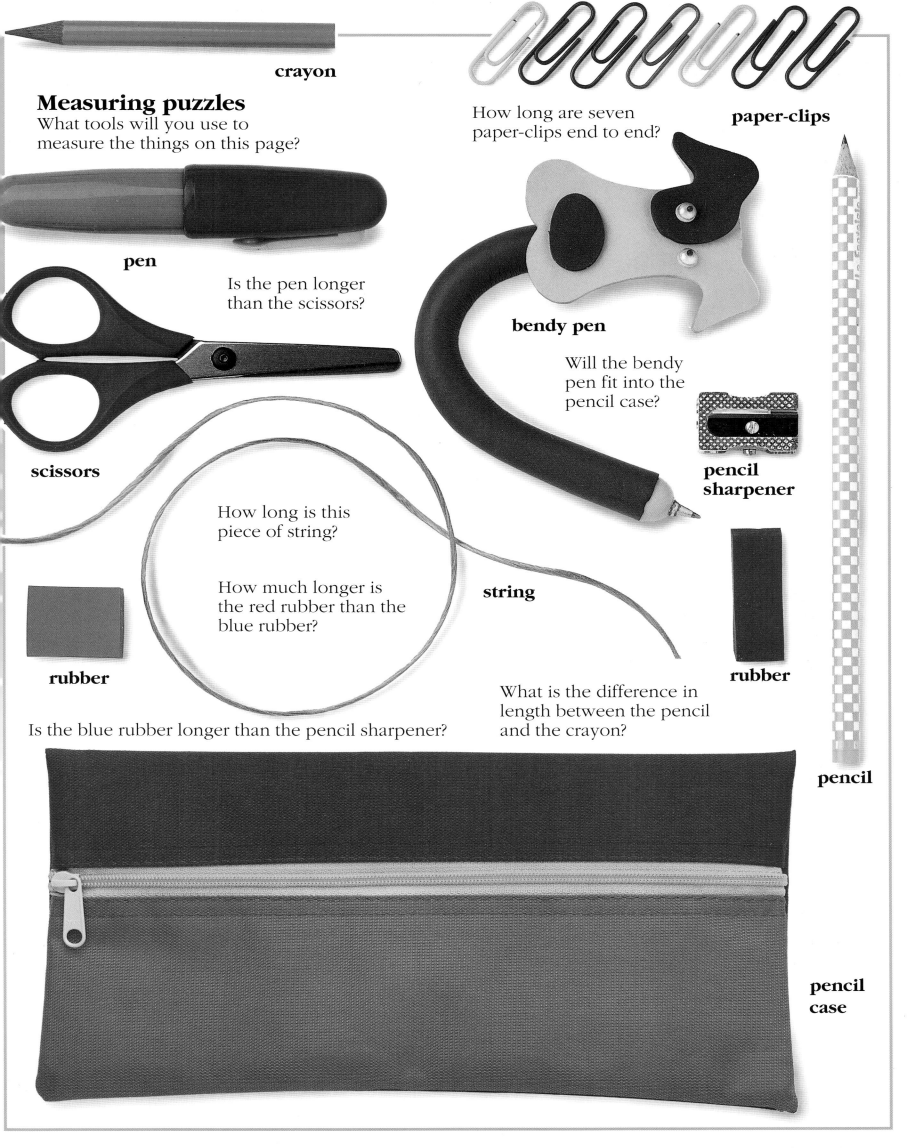

rubber

pencil

What is the difference in length between the pencil and the crayon?

Is the blue rubber longer than the pencil sharpener?

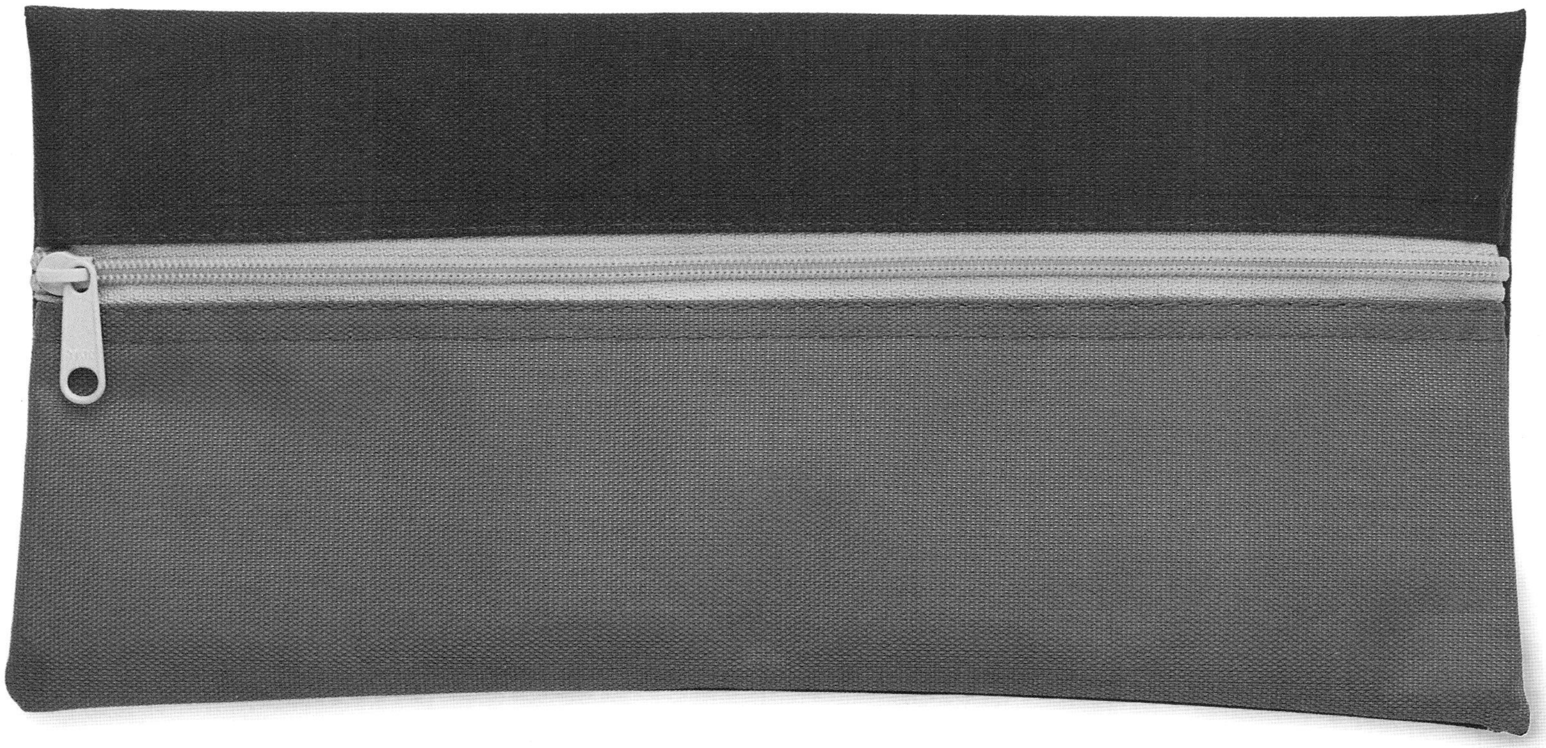

pencil case

Halves and quarters

When something is divided into equal parts, the parts are called **fractions**. Look at the apple examples here and then try to answer the puzzles below.

Halves

If an apple is cut into two equal parts, the pieces are called halves.

This is the symbol for one **half**.

$\frac{1}{2}$

$\frac{1}{2}$

Two halves make one whole.

$\frac{1}{4}$

This is the symbol for one **quarter**.

$\frac{1}{4}$

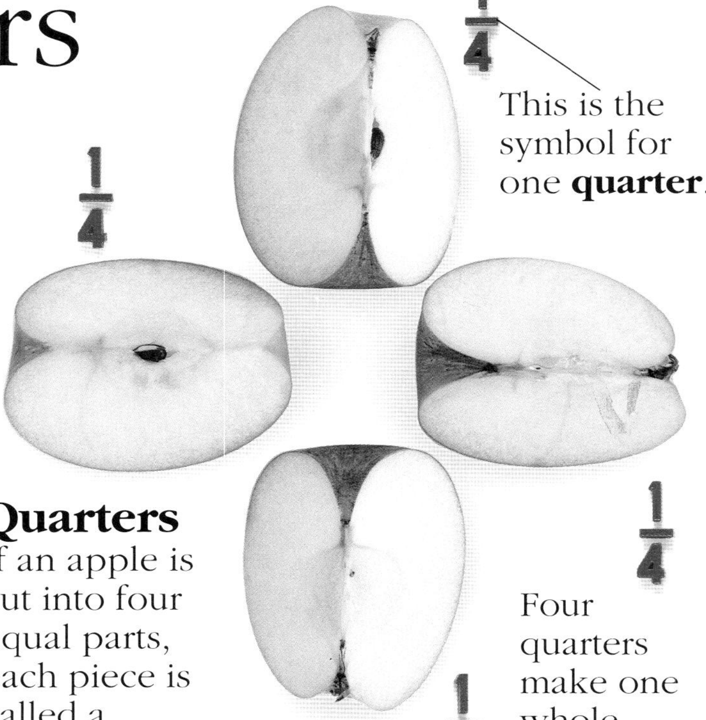

Quarters

If an apple is cut into four equal parts, each piece is called a quarter.

$\frac{1}{4}$

$\frac{1}{4}$

Four quarters make one whole.

Carrot

If a carrot is cut into four sticks, what fraction of the whole carrot is each stick?

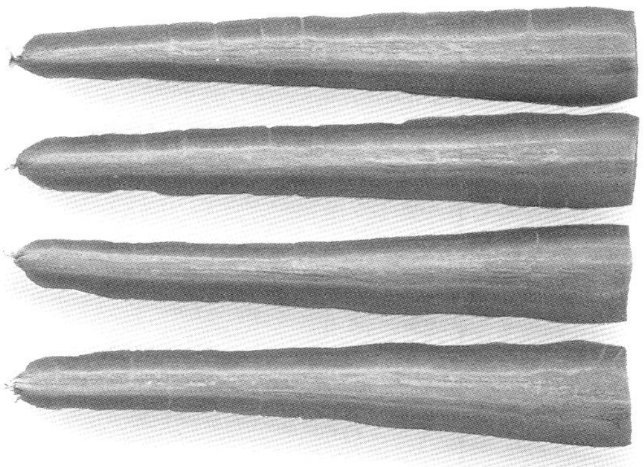

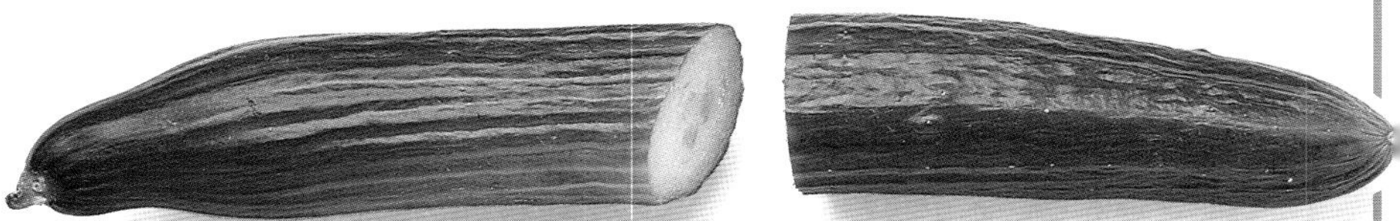

Cucumber

If a cucumber is cut into two equal parts, what is each piece called?

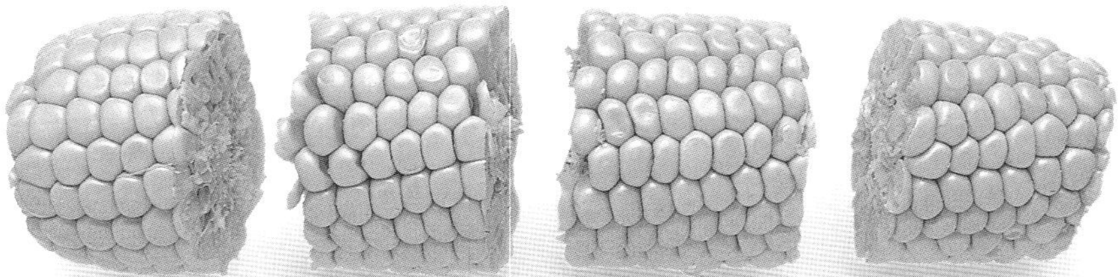

Banana desserts

How much banana is there in each dessert?

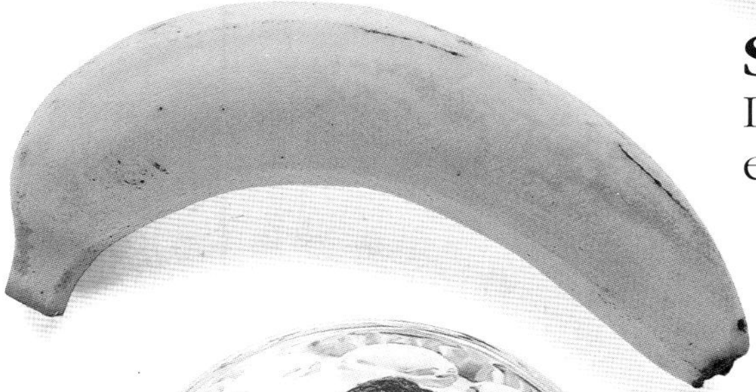

Sweetcorn

If three quarters of the sweetcorn is eaten what will be left?

Orange

If one quarter of an orange is left, how much has been eaten?

Bottles
The green bottle is half of the height of the red bottle. The blue bottle is half of the height of the green bottle.

Which bottle is quarter of the height of the red bottle?

Juice
Peter and Lian each had a full glass of juice. Peter has drunk half of his juice. How much has Lian drunk?

Tea
Here are eight tins of tea. If half of the tins are taken away, how many will be left?

If a quarter of the eight tins are taken away, how many tins are taken?

Fruit pie
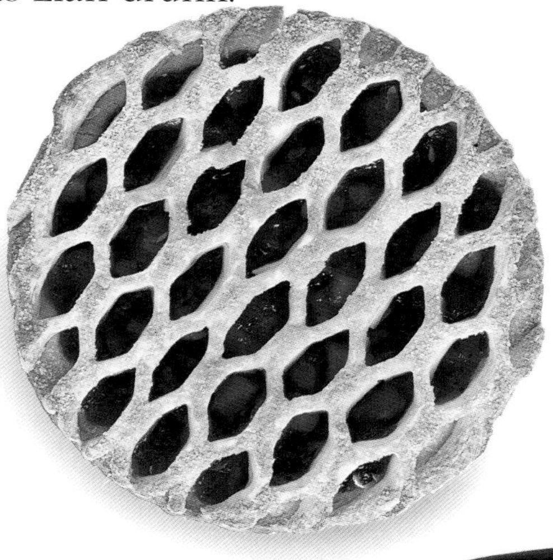

Six apples and eight spoons of flour were used to make this blackcurrant and apple pie.

How many apples and spoons of flour will be needed to make a pie half this size?

Biscuits

How many biscuits are there in half a pack?

Jugs
Look at these jugs of juice. Which jug is quarter full? How full are the other jugs?

Apple puzzle
Here are three apple halves. How many apples are there altogether?

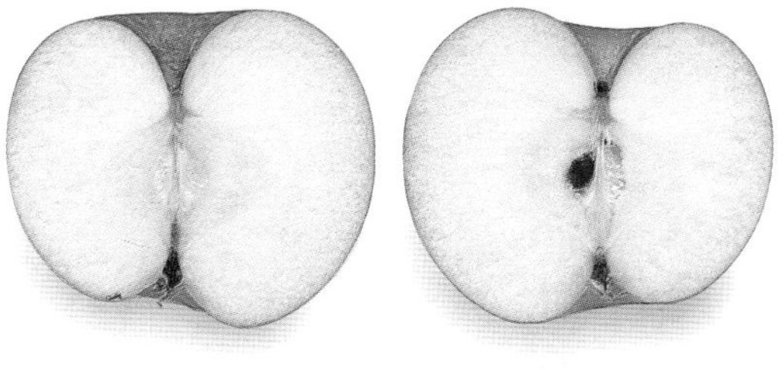

Moving around

When things turn around, or rotate, the amount of the turn can be measured in **degrees**.

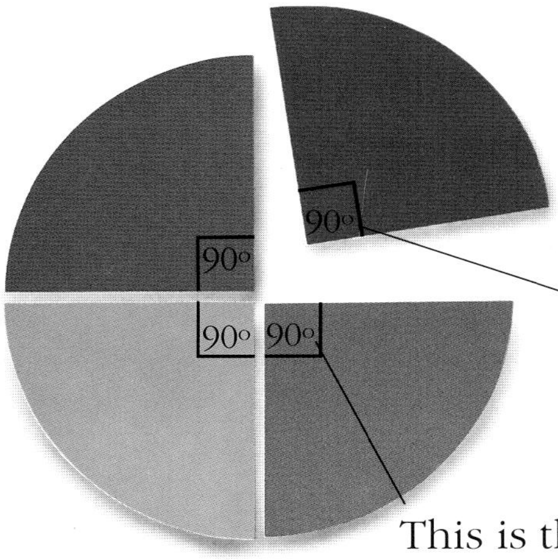

Angles

If a wheel turns all the way round, it turns through 360 degrees. A turn part of the way is called an **angle**.

A quarter turn is called a **right angle**. A right angle measures 90 degrees.

This is the symbol for degrees.

clockwise

anti-clockwise

Direction

The direction of a turn is called clockwise if it goes the same way as the hands on a clock.

Anti-clockwise means moving the opposite way round.

Which way do you turn a key to open a lock?

Right-angle tester

Make a right-angle tester by folding a piece of paper in half once, and then in half again.

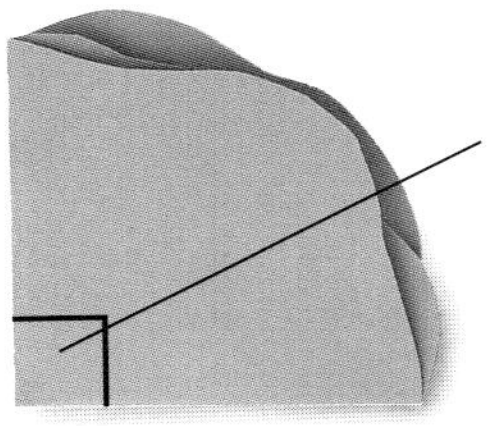

right angle

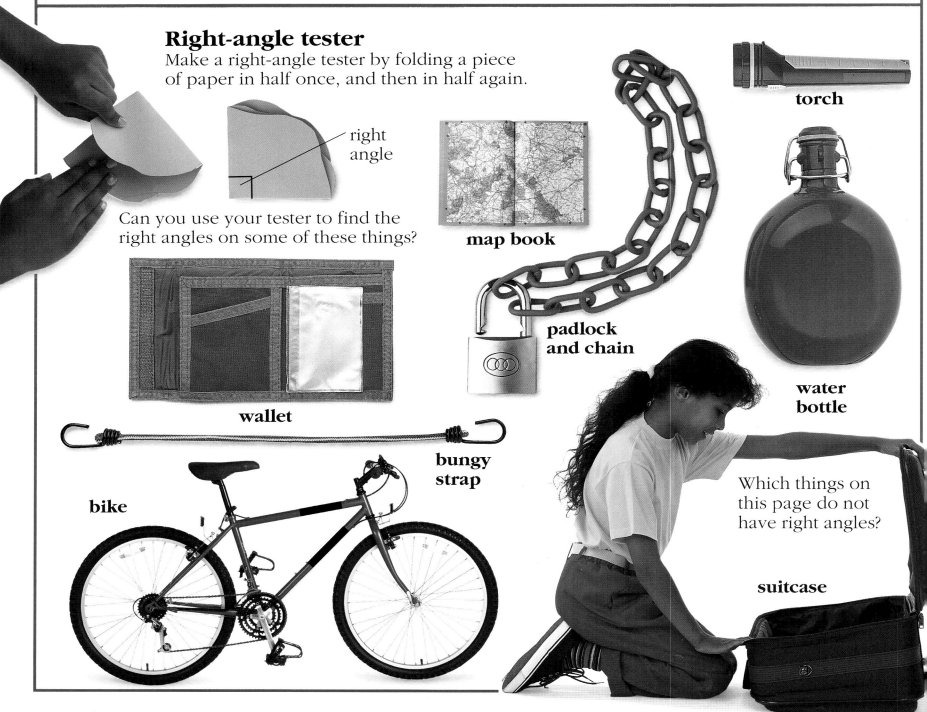

Can you use your tester to find the right angles on some of these things?

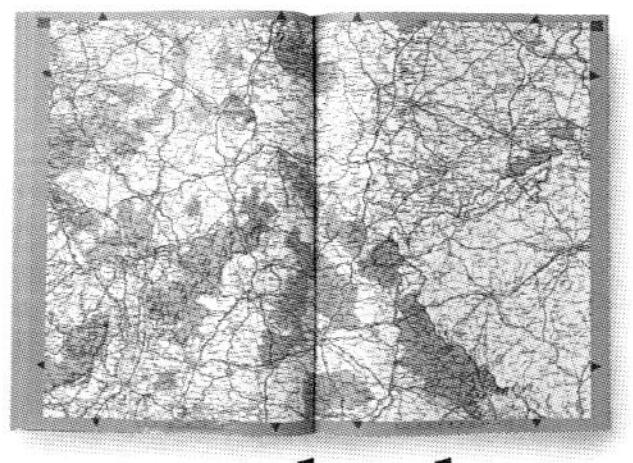

map book

padlock and chain

torch

water bottle

wallet

bungy strap

bike

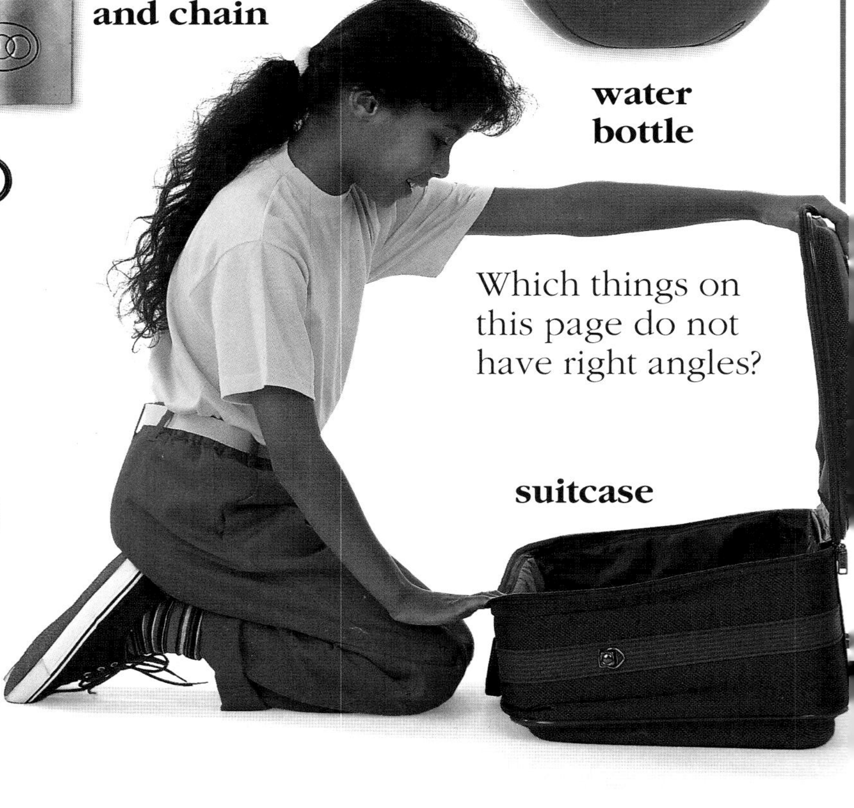

Which things on this page do not have right angles?

suitcase

Angle maze

Can you follow the yellow path and make only right-angled turns, to reach the treasure in the centre of the maze? How many right-angled turns do you have to make?

Can you find the shortest route out of the maze?
How many of the turns that you make are right angles?

Weight and volume

Weight is a measure of how heavy something is. **Volume** is about how much something will hold or how much space it takes up.

Solids

Solid things, such as washing powder, are sold by how much they weigh in **grams**, or **g** for short.

Both these packs weigh 500 grams but their volumes are different.

Does it matter whether you buy the bigger or the smaller box?

Liquids

Liquid things are usually sold by volume in **millilitres**, or **ml** for short.

These bottles will hold 250 millilitres of liquid. Which one only has 125 ml in it?

Toiletries

Which of these things is sold by weight and which by volume?

bubble bath

shampoo

bath salts

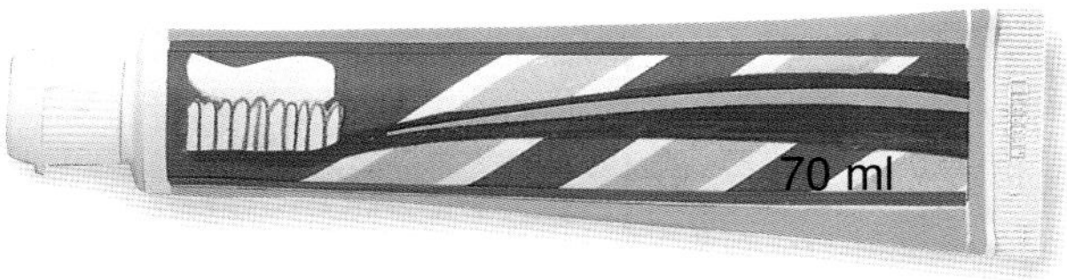

toothpaste

soap

talcum powder

Soap

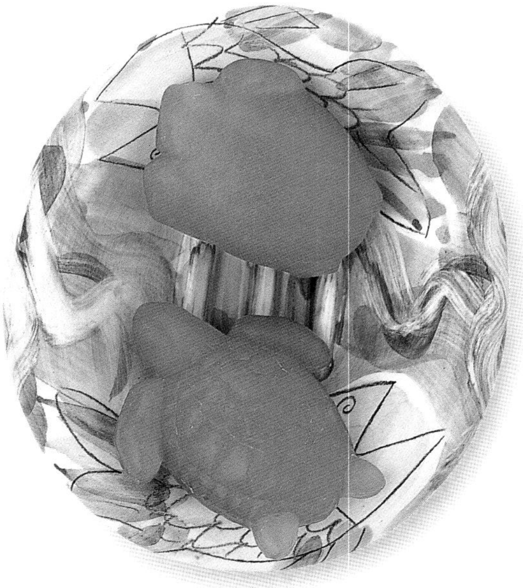

When you use a bar of soap, does its weight change?

What happens to its volume?

Sponge

Is a bath sponge heavier when it is wet, or when it is dry? Does its volume change when it gets wet?

Wash bag

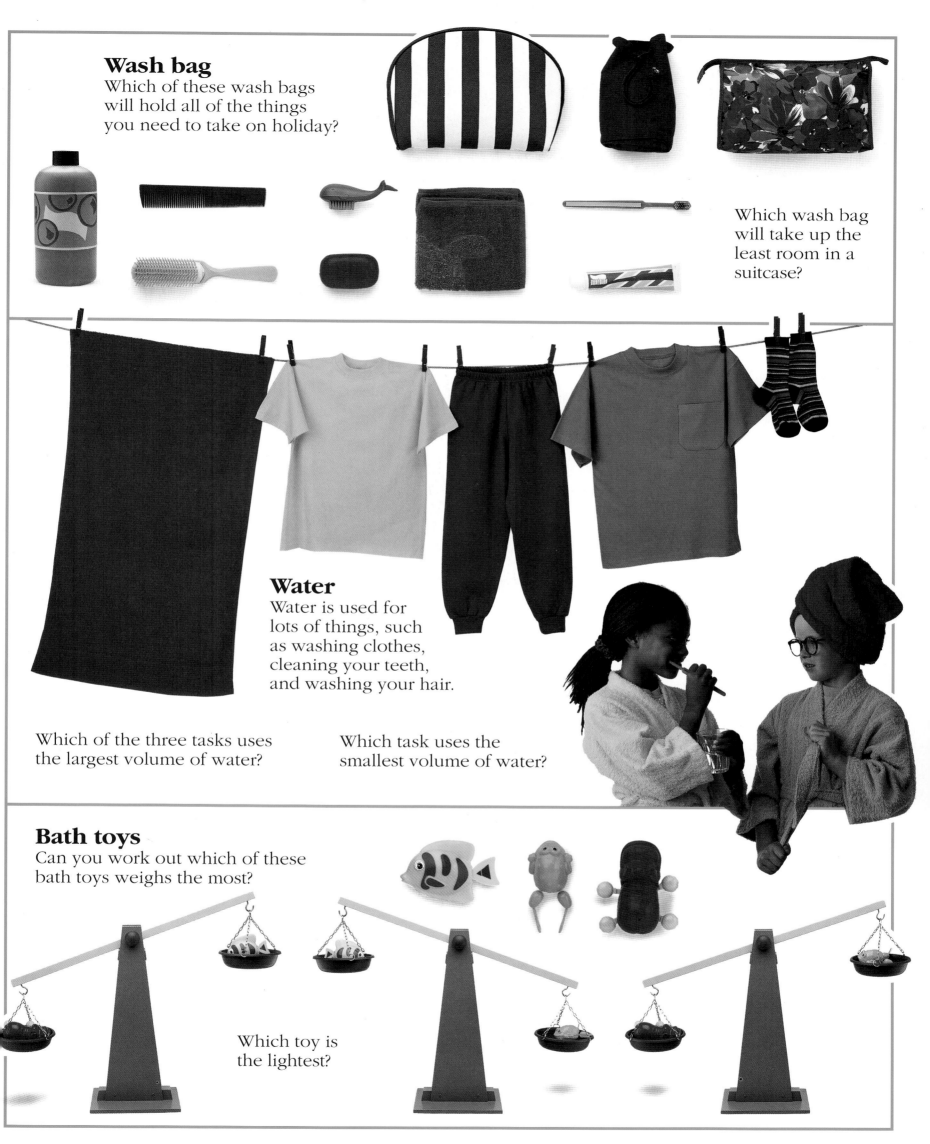

Which of these wash bags will hold all of the things you need to take on holiday?

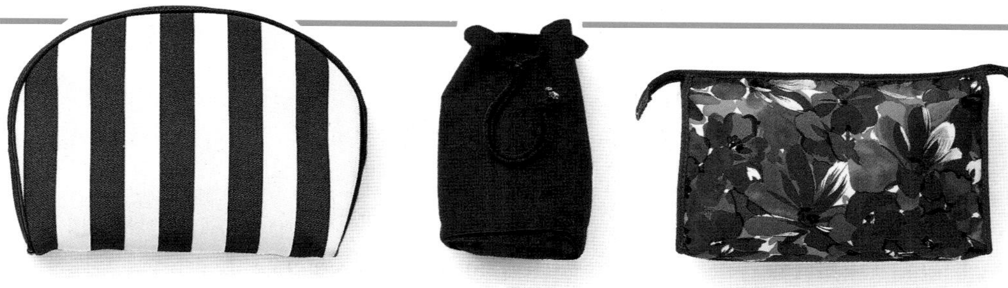

Which wash bag will take up the least room in a suitcase?

Water

Water is used for lots of things, such as washing clothes, cleaning your teeth, and washing your hair.

Which of the three tasks uses the largest volume of water?

Which task uses the smallest volume of water?

Bath toys

Can you work out which of these bath toys weighs the most?

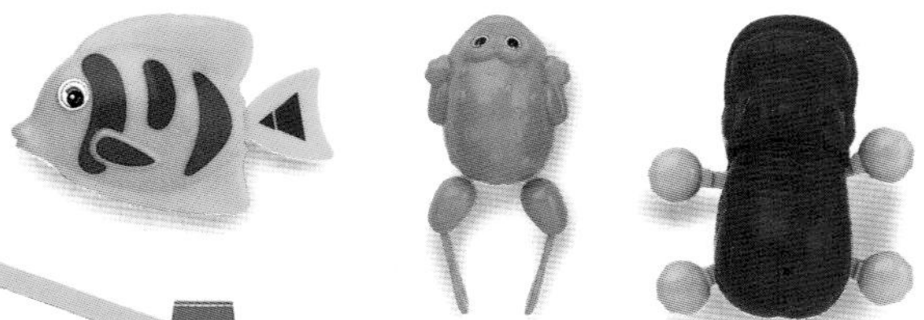

Which toy is the lightest?

Symmetry

An object shows symmetry either when it has two halves that match exactly, or if it looks the same when it is turned around.

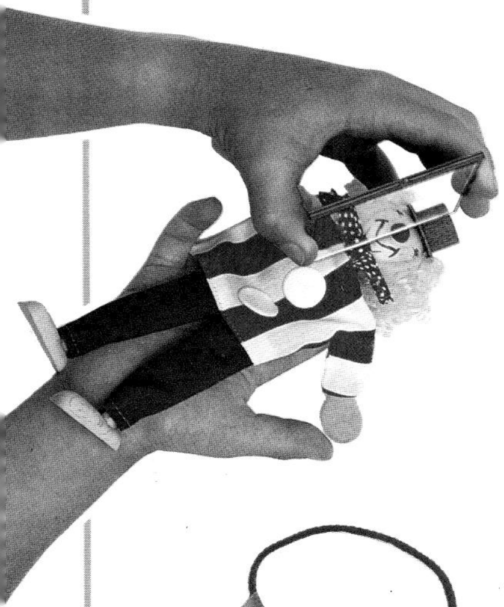

Mirror symmetry

Mirror symmetry is when both halves of things look the same. A mirror will help you to see where the two halves meet.

On flat shapes and pictures, the mirror line is called a **line of symmetry**. On objects it is called a **plane of symmetry**.

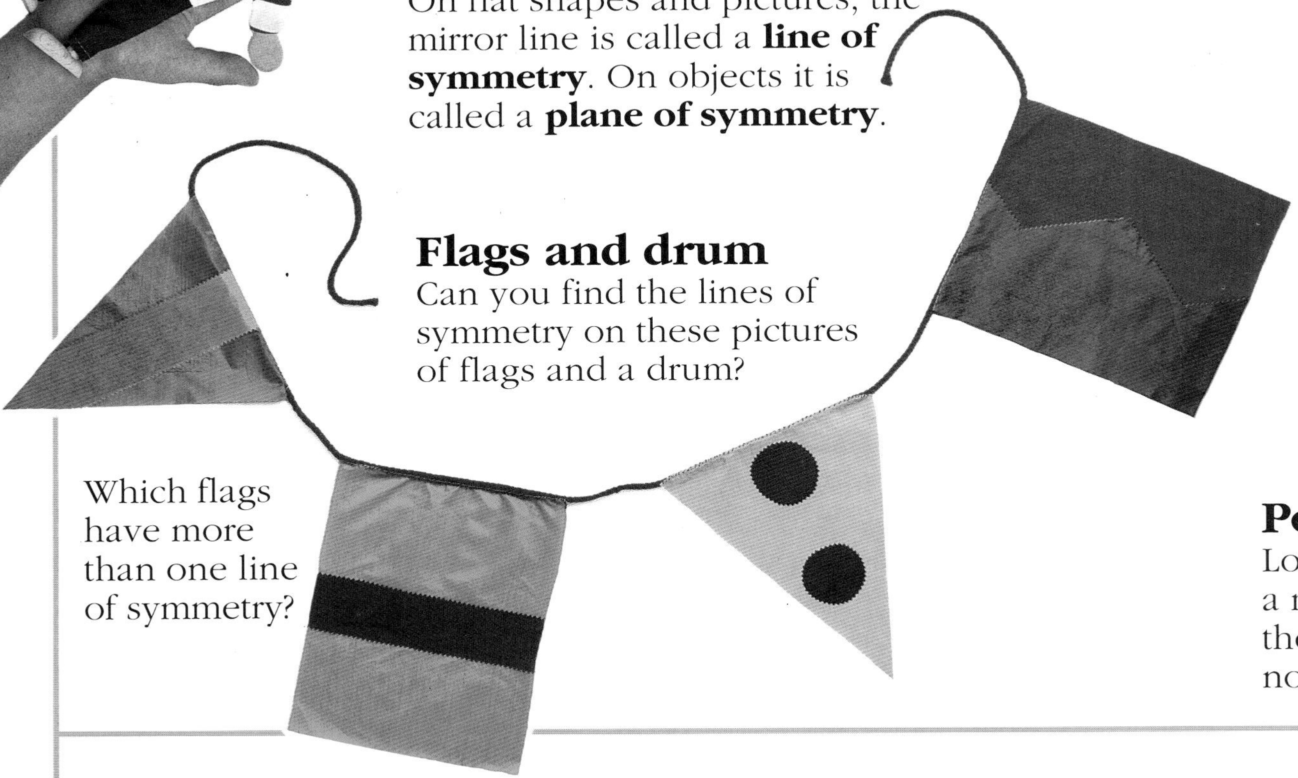

Flags and drum

Can you find the lines of symmetry on these pictures of flags and a drum?

Which flags have more than one line of symmetry?

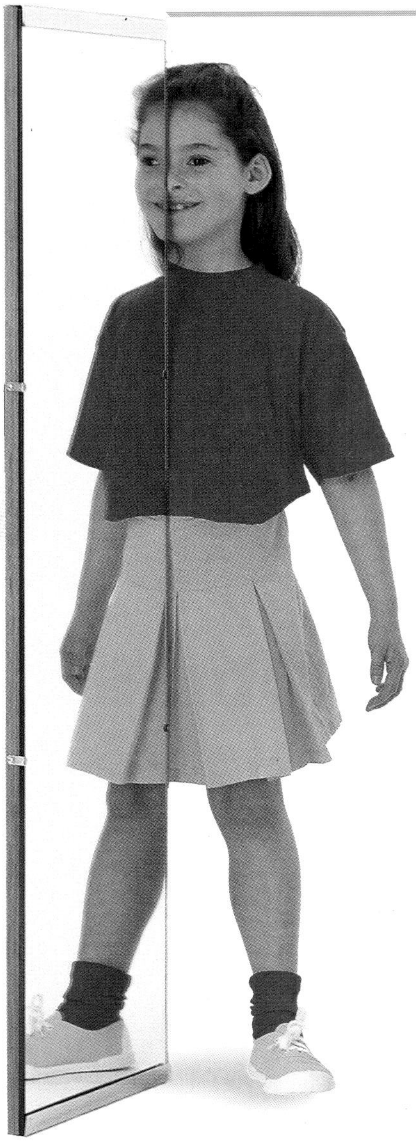

People

Look closely at a friend in a mirror like this. Although the two halves seem to match, no-one is exactly symmetrical.

Rotational symmetry

Things that look the same when turned around show rotational symmetry.

Flower

Does the flower show rotational symmetry?

Sun badge

Will the badge look different if you turn it around?

Windmill

Will the windmill look the same when its sails turn?

Symmetry puzzles

Can you say which things show mirror symmetry, and which ones show rotational symmetry?

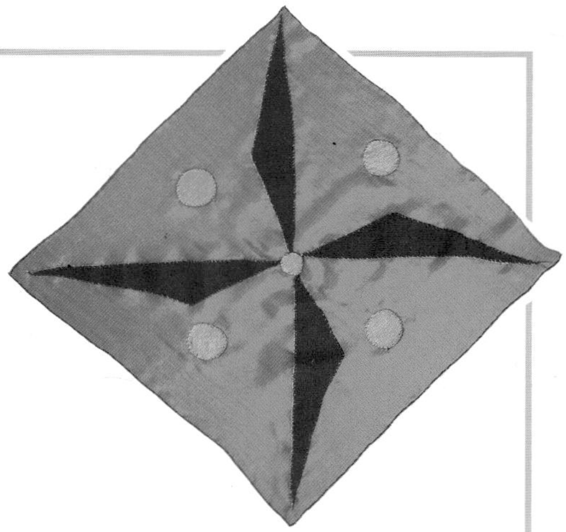

Some of the things show both kinds of symmetry. Can you see which ones?

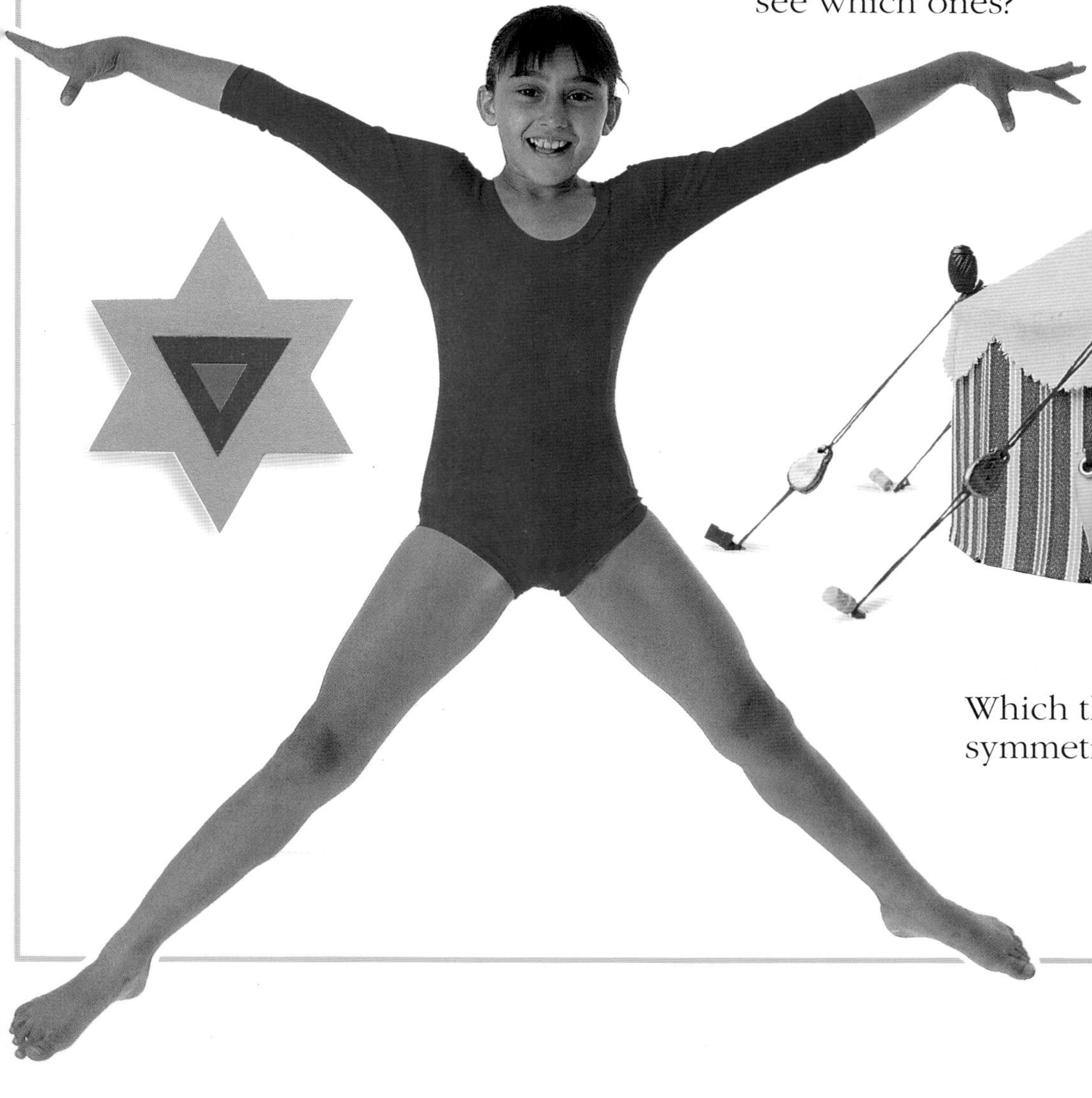

Which things are not symmetrical at all?

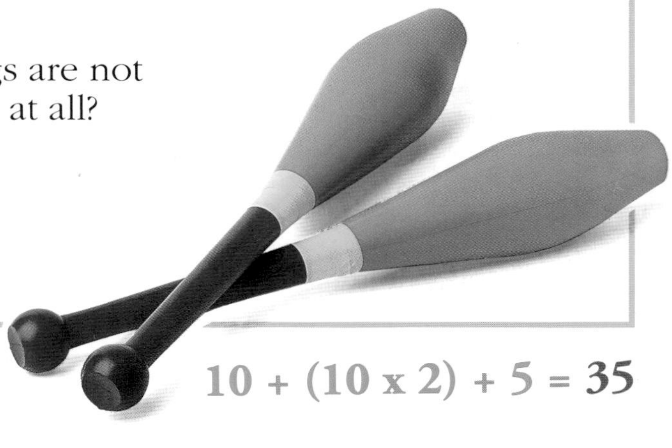

Time

The passing of time is described in centuries, years, months, weeks, days, hours, minutes, and seconds.

Did dinosaurs die out years or centuries ago?

Past time

Can you say how long ago these things happened?

How long ago did this year begin?

How many years ago were you one year old?

When did you last go out for a walk?

Present time

How much time do you think it takes for these things to happen?

How long does it take to grow some cress seeds?

How long does it take to count these flower petals?

If you throw some leaves into the air, how long do they take to fall?

How long does it take to make one page of a nature diary?

Future time

Will these things take minutes, hours, days, weeks, or years to happen?

How soon will a puppy grow up?

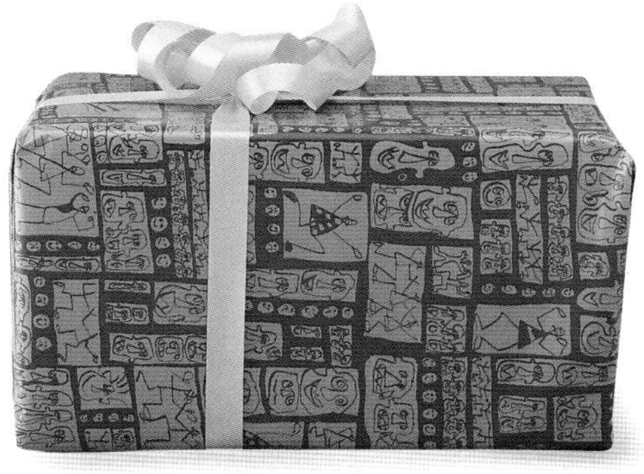

How soon will it be your birthday?

Fruit will go bad. How soon must these strawberries be eaten?

What time do you go to bed? How soon will it be bedtime?

Telling the time

The two hands on a clock move slowly around the clockface to tell you the time.

The hands on a clock always move this way, or clockwise.

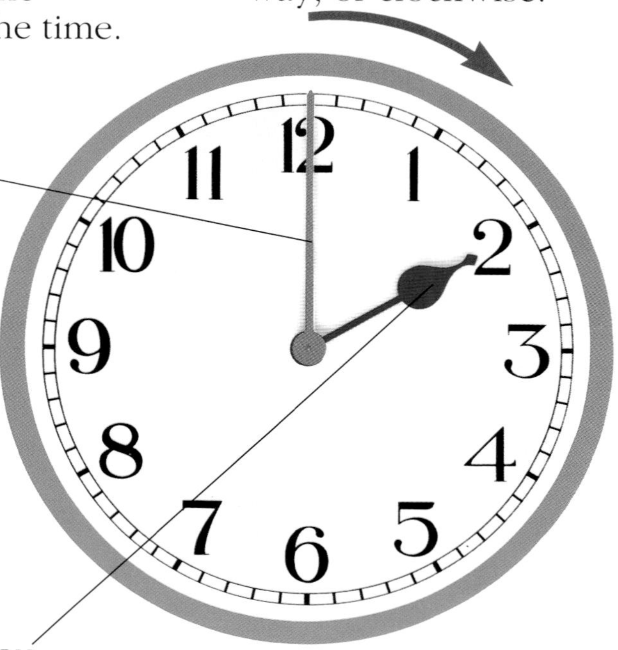

The long hand tells you the minutes. It takes one hour to go all round the clockface. When it points straight at the 12, it tells you that the time is something o'clock.

The short hand tells you the hour. It takes 12 hours to go all round the clockface. Here it points to the 2.

Two o'clock
This clock says it is two o'clock.

Quarter past two
When the long hand is on the 3, it has moved quarter of the way round the clockface.

Half past two
When the long hand is on the 6, it has moved half way round the clockface.

Quarter to three
When the long hand is on the 9, it has moved three-quarters of the way round the clockface. It has a quarter to go.

Minutes

There are 60 minutes in one hour. The long hand shows us how many minutes have gone by.

The long hand has gone round 55 minutes. There are 5 minutes of the hour to go.

There are 5 minutes between each number on a clockface.

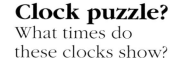

The short hand is nearly on the 9.

Five to nine
Together the hands tell you that the time is 5 minutes to 9 o'clock.

Clock puzzle?

What times do these clocks show?

Picture graphs

The picture charts on these pages are called **graphs**. Can you find out the answers to the number questions by looking at the graphs?

Summer holidays

This graph shows where some children spent their summer holidays.

How many children went to the mountains? Which was the most popular place to go for a holiday?

Weekend fun

Here is a graph showing the different things that some children did at the weekend.

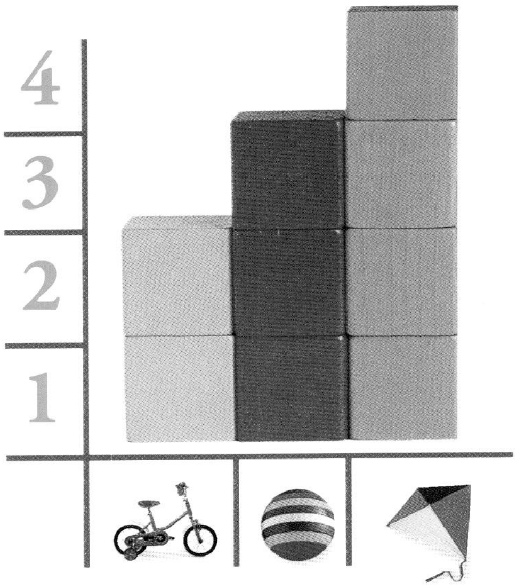

How many children played ball?
How many children rode bicycles?
Which activity did most children do?

Colourful beads

How many beads of each colour do you need to make this necklace?

How many beads do you need altogether? Use the graph to help you.

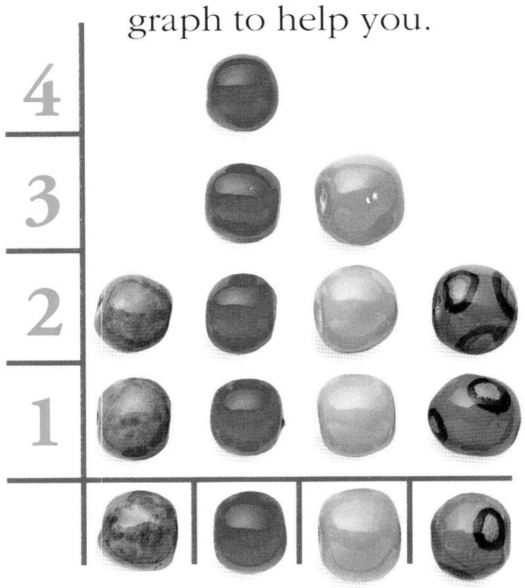

Tall and short

This graph uses footprints to show how tall these children are. Their heights are marked on the graph with a green line.

Who is five footprints tall?
How many footprints tall is Tom?
How many footprints tall is the shortest child?

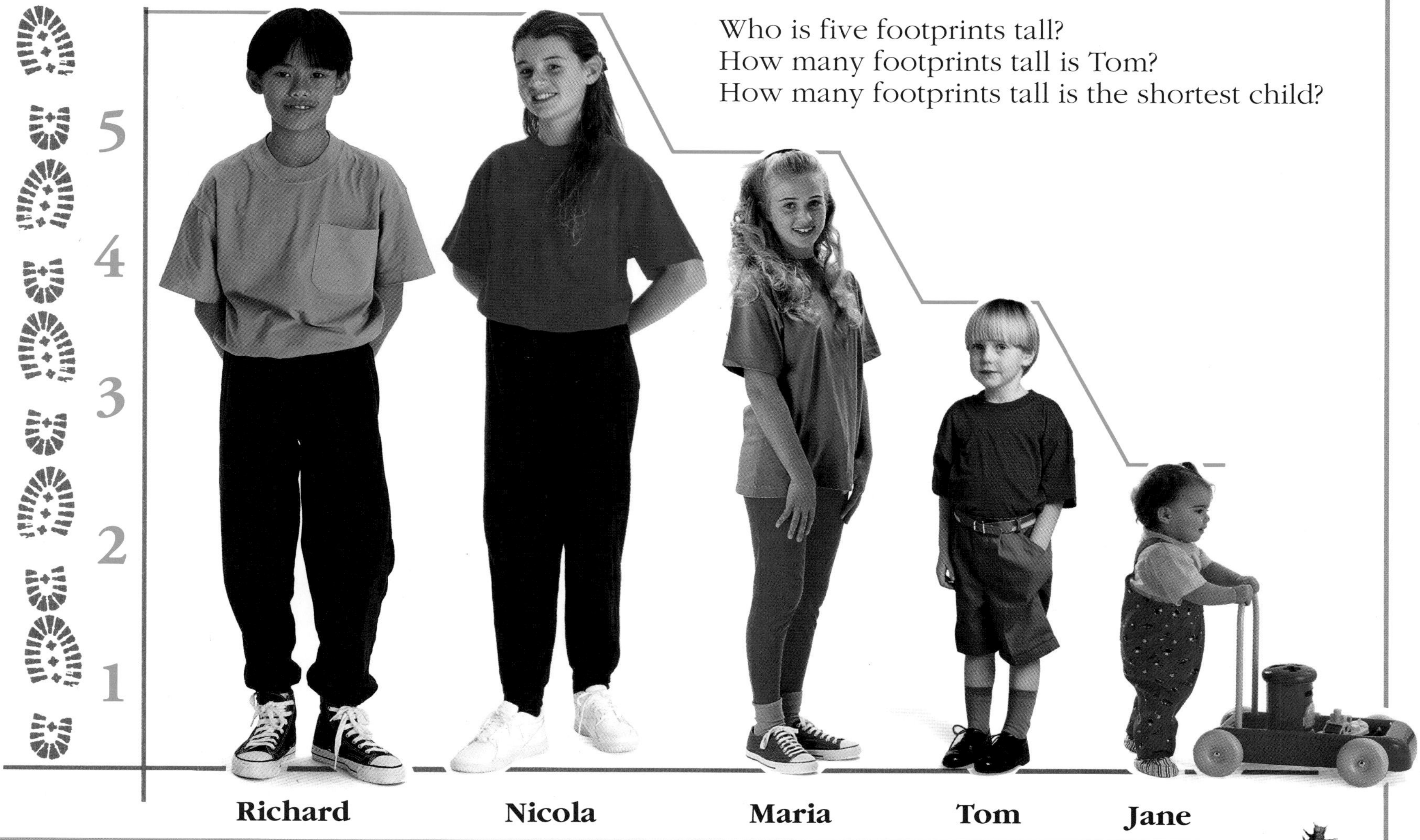

Happy pets

Which pet has the most treats to eat?

Does the parrot have more treats than the dog?

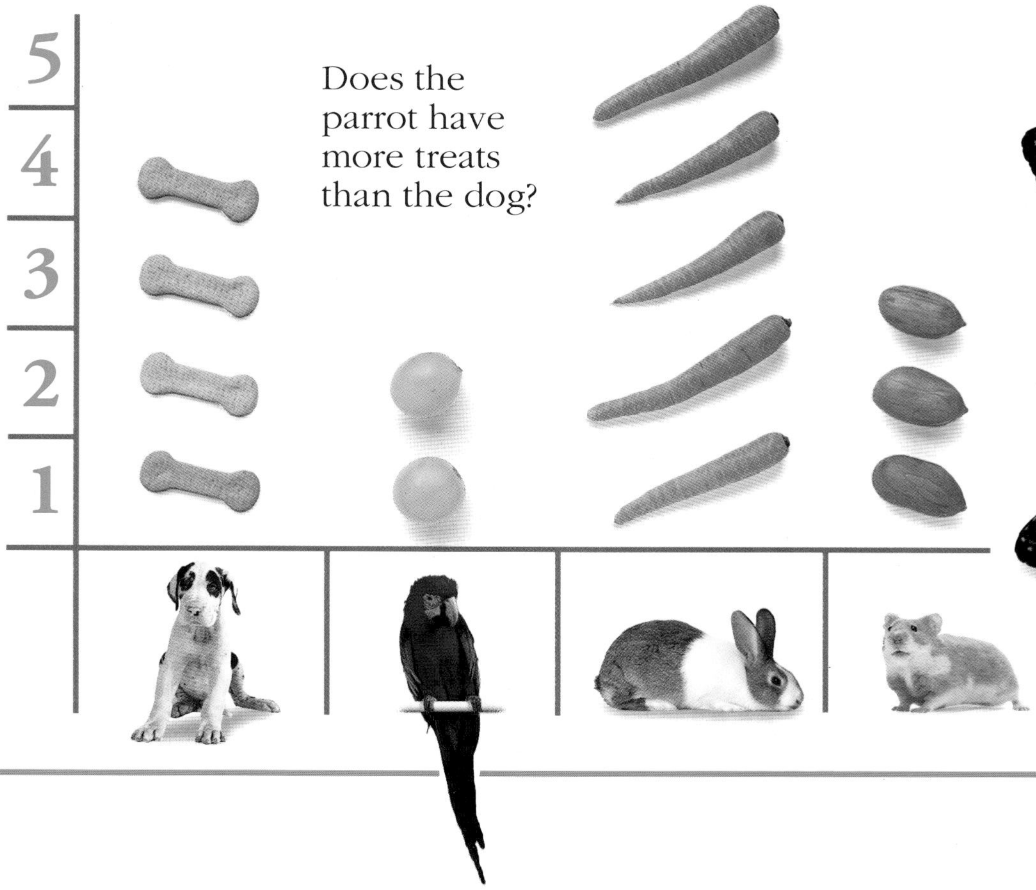

Creepy crawlies

How many beetles, butterflies, and caterpillars can you find on this page?

Can you draw your own graph to show the answers?

Calculators

A calculator is a machine that you can use to work out, or calculate, the answers to additions, divisions, subtractions, and multiplications.

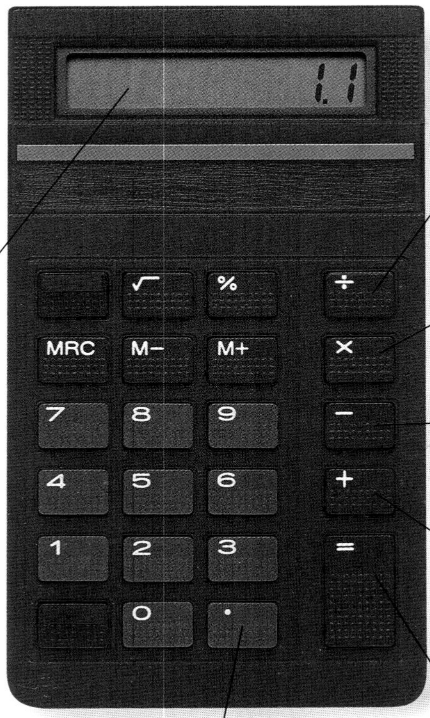

Calculator

Switch on your calculator. What appears on the screen when you press some of the number keys? Can you find the button that clears the screen?

This is a **decimal point**

Press the 1 button. Now **key in** the decimal point. Press the 1 again. Do you get this number?

Decimals

Numbers after a decimal point are parts, or fractions, of a whole number. One number after the point shows parts of a whole number in tenths. Two numbers after the point show the fractions in hundredths.

Calculator shopping

Can you add up some prices with a calculator? Try this example first.

+

= £5.48

Switch on the calculator and key in 3. Now key in the decimal point followed by 2, then 4.

Press the add key. Now key in 2.24 and press the equals key.

Does the screen show 5.48? Now clear the screen.

Price tags

Can you add these prices together?

+

+

= ?

+

+

+

= ?

Shopping puzzle

Can you work out the answers to the following questions? Use your calculator to check your work.

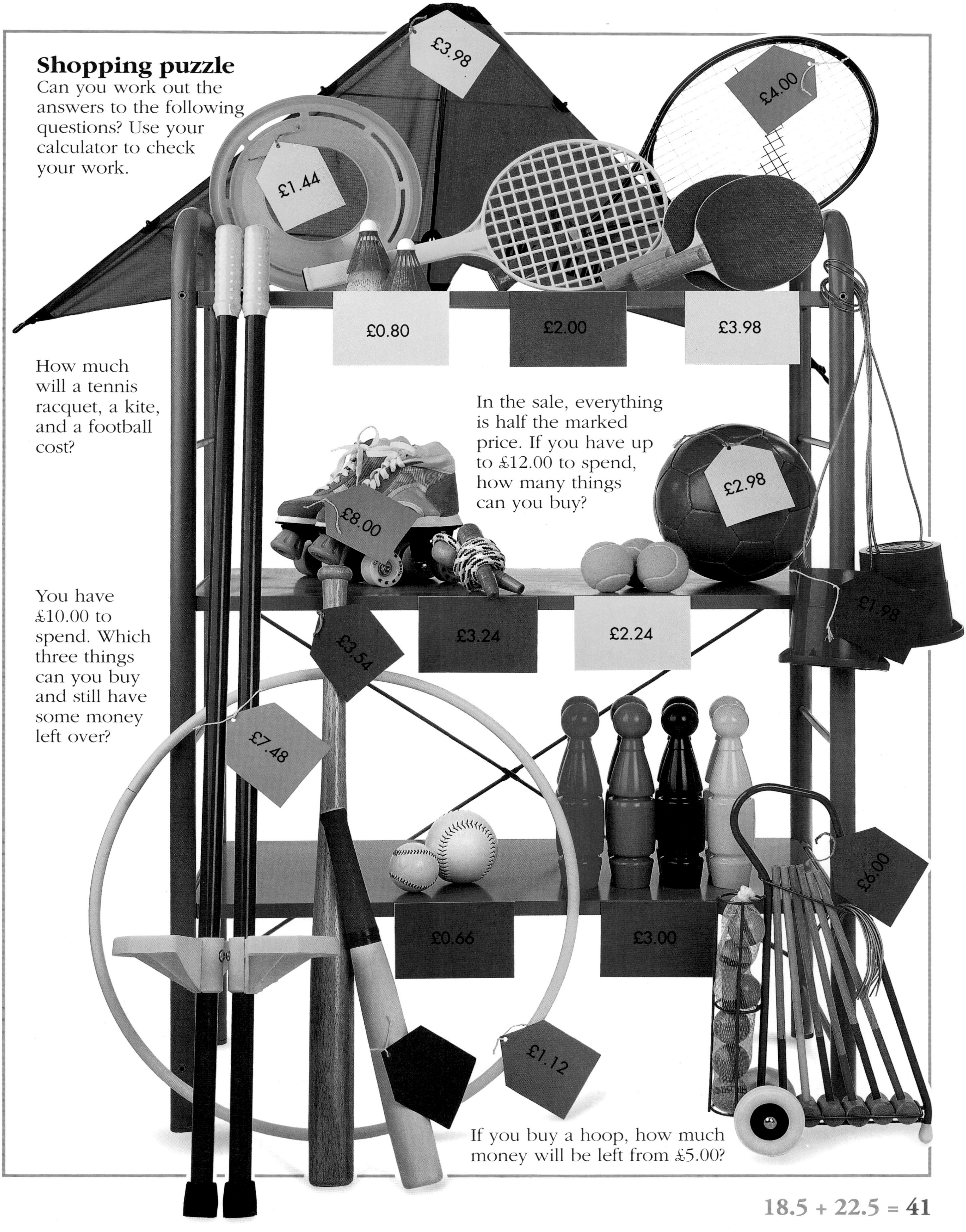

How much will a tennis racquet, a kite, and a football cost?

In the sale, everything is half the marked price. If you have up to £12.00 to spend, how many things can you buy?

You have £10.00 to spend. Which three things can you buy and still have some money left over?

If you buy a hoop, how much money will be left from £5.00?

Figure it out

Here are lots of puzzles for you to try and find out how much you know.

Shapes

How many of these shapes can you name?

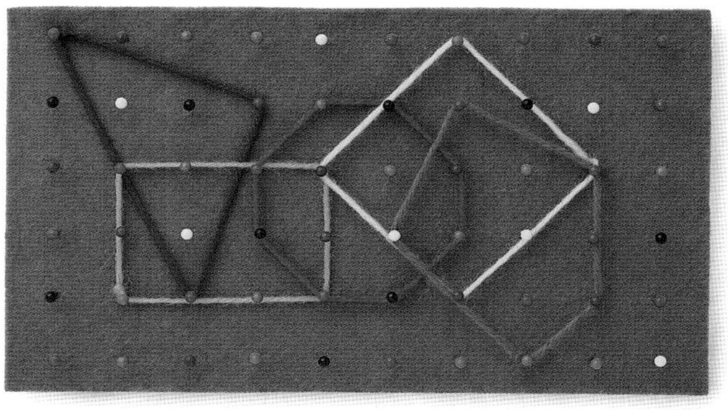

Calculator challenge

Use a calculator to try these divisions.

$$1 \div 2 = ?$$

$$1 \div 4 = ?$$

Do you get the answers you expect?

Birthdays

Liz is 1 year and 10 days younger than Sean. How old will Sean be on Liz's 8th birthday?

Angles

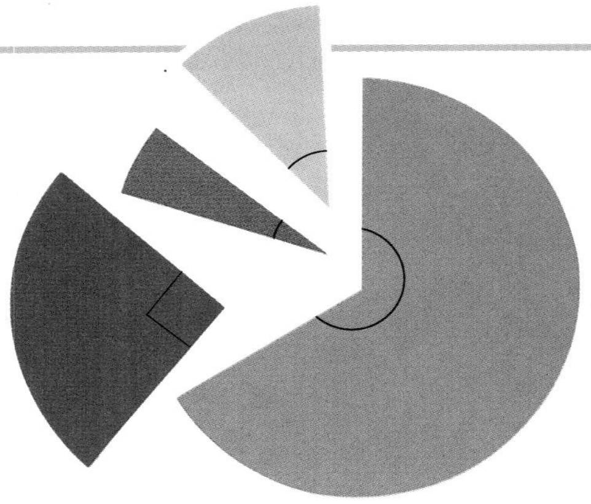

Which angle is a right angle?

How many degrees are there in a right angle?

Measuring length

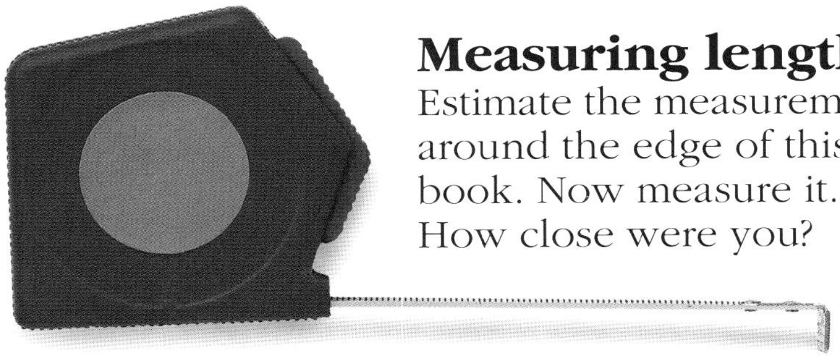

Estimate the measurement around the edge of this book. Now measure it. How close were you?

Symmetry

What could you do to the pattern on this card to make it symmetrical in two directions?

Tessellating face

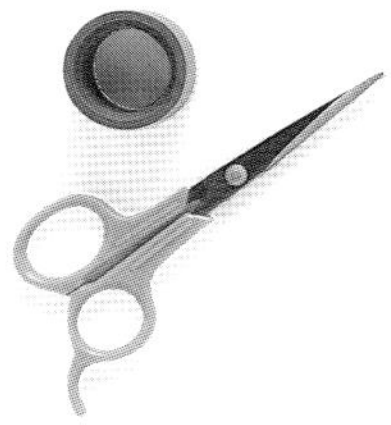

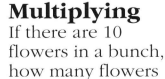

Can you make a tessellating face shape with a piece of cardboard, cut like this?

Multiplying

If there are 10 flowers in a bunch, how many flowers will there be in 5 bunches?

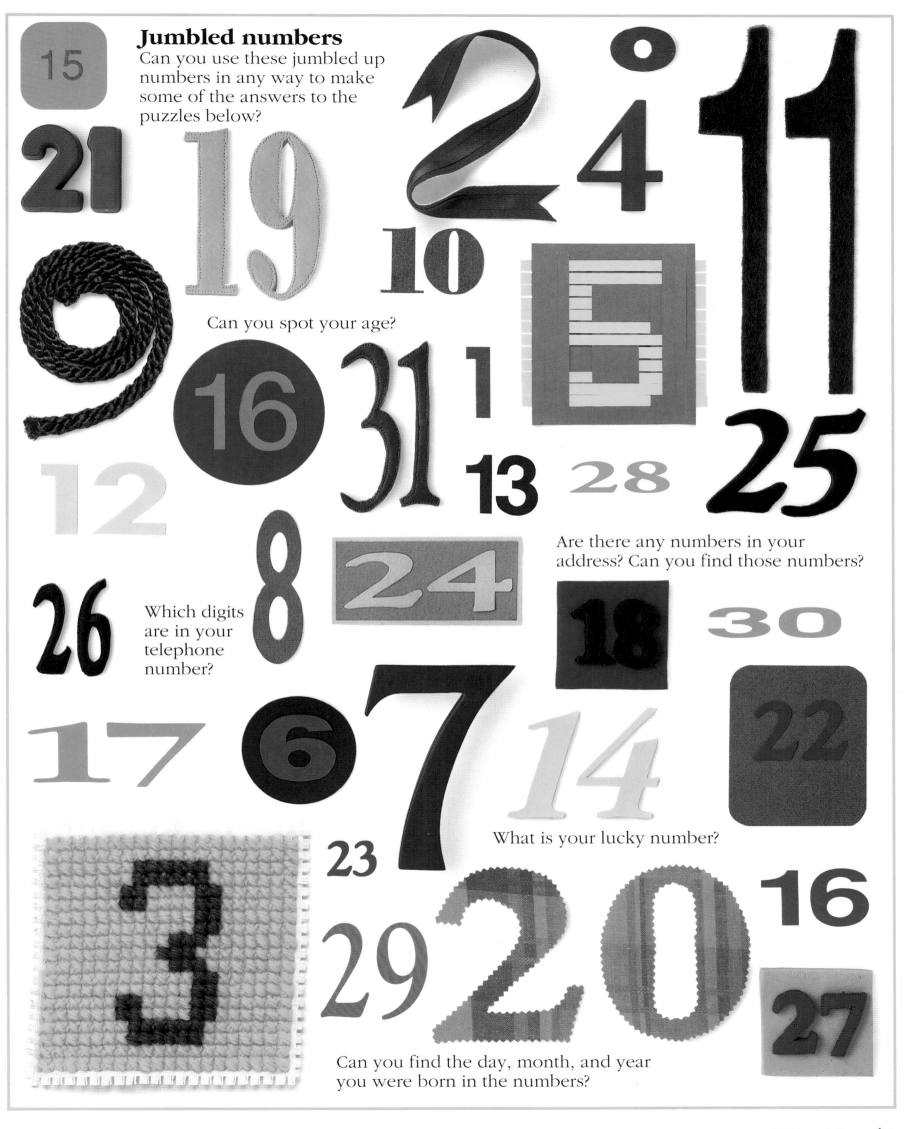

Jumbled numbers

Can you use these jumbled up numbers in any way to make some of the answers to the puzzles below?

Can you spot your age?

Which digits are in your telephone number?

Are there any numbers in your address? Can you find those numbers?

What is your lucky number?

Can you find the day, month, and year you were born in the numbers?

Number facts

Which of these number facts do you know?

Numbers of musicians

There are words to describe the number of musicians in a group.

1 = soloist
2 = duo
3 = trio
4 = quartet
5 = quintet
6 = sextet
7 = septet
8 = octet

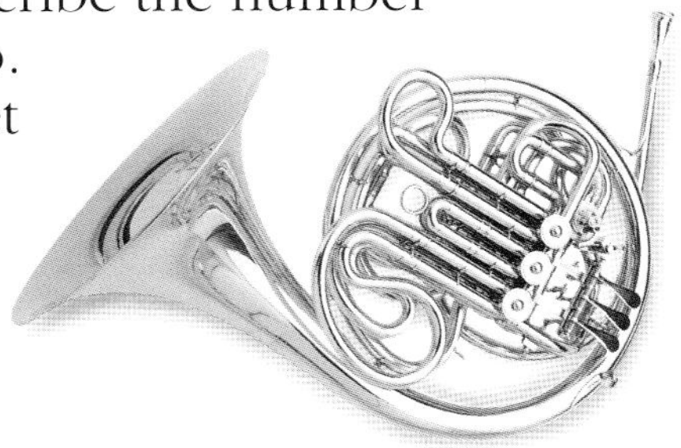

Babies

If brothers, sisters, or brothers and sisters are born on the same day and year there are words to describe them.

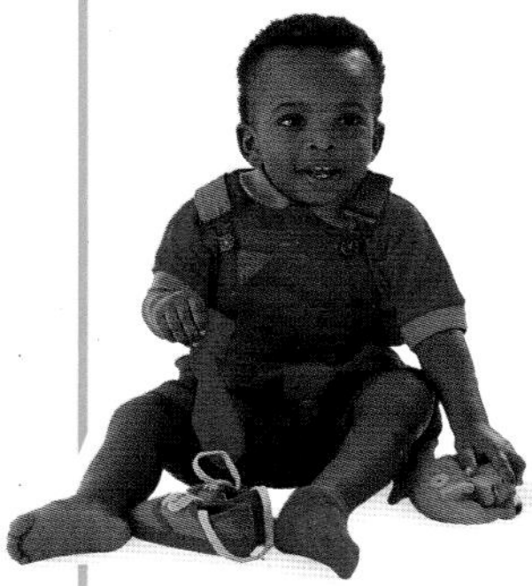

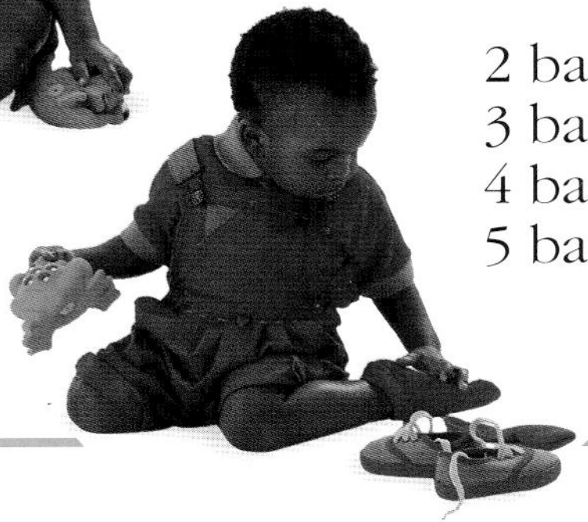

2 babies = twins
3 babies = triplets
4 babies = quadruplets
5 babies = quintuplets

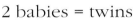

Time facts

There are 60 seconds in a minute.
There are 60 minutes in an hour.
There are 24 hours in a day.
There are 7 days in a week.
There are 52 weeks in a year.
There are 12 months in a year.
There are 100 years in a century.
There are 1000 years in a millenium.

Leap year

There are $365\frac{1}{4}$ days in a year. We say there are 365 days in a normal year and then every fourth year we add an extra day and call it a leap year.

Big numbers

To make very big numbers easier to read, we leave a space between each group of three zeros, or put a comma between each group.

ten	10
hundred	100
thousand	1000
ten thousand	10 000
hundred thousand	100 000
million	1 000 000
billion	1 000 000 000 000
trillion	1 000 000 000 000 000 000
googol	10 000 000 000 000 000 000 000 000 000 000 000 000 000 000 000 000 000 000

How many zeros are there in a googol?

Glossary

add (+) To put two or more numbers together to find the total. This type of sum is called an **addition**. (page 10)

angle The amount of turn, measured in degrees. (page 30)

centimetre (cm) A measure of length. There are 100 centimetres in 1 metre. (page 26)

circumference The distance round a circular shape. (page 26)

decimal point (.) A sign to show that the numbers after it are parts of a whole number. (page 40)

degree (°) Angles are measured in degrees. There are 360° in a complete turn. (page 30)

digit A symbol used in writing numbers. 0, 1, 2, 3, 4, 5, 6, 7, 8, and 9 are all digits. (page 14)

divide by (÷) To share things out into equal parts. This type of calculation is called a **division**. (page 16)

equal to (=) This means "the same as". (page 10)

face A flat surface of a solid shape. (page 24)

fraction Part of a whole. A bite from a pear is a fraction of the pear. (page 28)

gram (g) A measure of weight. There are 1000 grams in 1 kilogram. (page 32)

graph A chart showing number information. (page 38)

half When something is cut into two equal parts, each piece is a half. (page 28)

key in To press the keys or control buttons on a calculator or computer keyboard to put numbers, letters, or commands into the machine. (page 40)

kilogram (kg) A measure of weight. In some countries, things such as flour and sugar are sold in bags that weigh 1 kilogram. (page 32)

line of symmetry An imaginary line down or across a flat shape, or picture, where it could be cut into two matching halves. (page 34)

litre (l) A measure of volume for liquids. (page 32)

lots of Groups of things. 4 lots of 5 means 4 groups with 5 things in each group. (page 16)

metre (m) A measure of length. (page 26)

millilitre (ml) A small measure of volume. There are 1000 millilitres in 1 litre. (page 32)

millimetre (mm) A small measure of length. There are 10 millimetres in 1 centimetre. (page 26)

multiply by (x) To add the same number lots of times. 2+2+2, or 3 lots of 2, is the same as 3 multiplied by 2. This calculation is called a **multiplication**. (page 16)

net The shape that a solid shape would make if it were opened out and laid flat. (page 25)

plane of symmetry An imaginary line down or across the middle of a solid object, where it could be cut into two matching halves. (page 34)

quarter When something is cut into four equal parts, each piece is a quarter. (page 28)

right angle A turn of 90 degrees. (page 30)

set A group of things that go together in some way. (page 8)

subtract (–) To take one number away from another number to find how many are left. This calculation is called a **subtraction**. (page 10)

symbol A sign which shows some information in a simple or short way. (page 16)

take away (–) To put aside, or remove. This is another way to say "subtract". (page 10)

tessellate To fit flat shapes together with no spaces left between them. Tessellations can be made by using one, two, or more shapes together, again and again. (page 23)

three-dimensional (3-D) Solid, with height, width, and depth. A cube is a 3-D shape. (page 24)

two-dimensional (2-D) Flat, with height and width but with no depth or thickness. A square is a 2-D shape. (page 22)

volume The amount of space something takes up, or how much it holds. A bath towel has a bigger volume than a face cloth. A bath tub will hold more water than a bowl. (page 32)

Acknowledgements

Additional photography: Paul Bricknell, Andy Crawford, Philip Dowell, Michael Dunning, Andreas Einsiedel, Jo Foord, Dave King, Stephen Oliver, Daniel Pangbourne, Susanna Price, Tim Ridley, Karl Shone, Steve Shott, and Jerry Young. **Models:** Donks Models, Simon Money, and Paul Scannell. **Jacket design:** Chris Branfield. **Additional design:** Mandy Earey and Peter Radcliffe. Dorling Kindersley would like to thank the following for appearing in this book: Annette Afflick, Sean Allkins, Jason Archie, Marvin Campbell, Dean Cook, Ebru Djemal, Hugo Edwards, Josey Edwards, Hêloise Evans, Sophie Gamba, Kelly Gomez, Tony Hans, Samantha Ho, Emel Karacan, Daniel Lawrence, Andrew Linnet, Yuksel Mustafa, Keat Ng, Lian Ng, Charlotte Raynsford, Jack Richards, Jeremy Smith, Barnaby Spiegel, Naomi Terry, Melanie Voice, Georgette Walford, Shaun White, and Michele Woolf.

00 000 000 000 000 000 000 000 000 000 000 000 000 000 000

51	52	53	54	55
61	62	63	64	65
71	72	73	74	75
81	82	83	84	85
91	92	93	94	95